Do you have the courage to earn half a million dollars a year?

Discover The "Trading S.W.T" method that is leading the wolves of wall street to earn staggering figures during this period of crisis.

Warren B. Kratter

Copyright 2020 - All rights reserved.

The content contained within this book may not be reproduced, duplicated or transmitted without direct written permission from the author or the publisher.

Under no circumstances will any blame or legal responsibility be held against the publisher, or author, for any damages, reparation, or monetary loss due to the information contained within this book. Either directly or indirectly.

Legal Notice:

This book is copyright protected. This book is only for personal use. You cannot amend, distribute, sell, use, quote or paraphrase any part, or the content within this book, without the consent of the author or publisher.

Disclaimer Notice:

Please note the information contained within this document is for educational and entertainment purposes only. All effort has been executed to present accurate, up to date, and reliable, complete information. No warranties of any kind are declared or implied. Readers acknowledge that the author is not engaging in the rendering of legal, financial, medical or professional advice. The content within this book has been derived from various sources. Please consult a licensed professional before attempting any techniques outlined in this book.

By reading this document, the reader agrees that under no circumstances is the author responsible for any losses, direct or indirect, which are incurred as a result of the use of information contained within this document, including, but not limited to, — errors, omissions, or inaccuracies.

TABLE OF CONTENT

Introduction Swing trading..114

Chapter 1 How Swing Trading Works...116

Chapter 2 Tools And Platforms..126

Chapter 3 Financial Instruments For Swing...............................138

Chapter 4 Risk And Account Management................................149

Chapter 5 Fundamental Analysis...158

Chapter 6 Technical Analysis Charting Basics..........................168

Chapter 7 Swing-Trading Rules 179

Chapter 8 The Swing Trader Mindset 185

Chapter 9 Swing Trading Strategies. 195

Chapter 10 Intermediate and Advanced Trading Strategies 202

Chapter 11 Trend 212

Conclusion...216

Introduction Swing Trading

Swing trading is an exciting opportunity for small and individual investors to make an income on the stock market.

In fact, swing trading is a general technique that can be used to earn income from stocks, commodities, and even on Forex. You can think of swing trading as a middle ground between long term investing and day trading.

We will explore the similarities and differences along with specific details in the book, but, for now, you can think of swing trading as day trading but over longer time frames and with far less risk.

Rather than trying to make money off of your trades in the matter of a few hours, with swing trading your goal is to make money off changing share prices over time frames ranging from days to many weeks.

A swing trader doesn't need to sit at his computer watching the stock markets all day long, although you certainly can if that is an option for you and you like doing it. Swing traders can also start small and grow their business over time.

Day trading involves lots of upfront costs instead. The word "business" should catch your eye. In short, swing trading is a business. Rather than building a long-term retirement account, swing trading is all about earning profits in the short term.

While substantial profits are possible, it's not a get-rich-quick scheme and although it can be done on a part-time basis, we want you to start thinking of swing trading as a business from this point forward.

The goal is to earn profits, and you can use those profits as ordinary income if you like or reinvest them to build your retirement account or some combination of the two.

That is entirely up to you. But keep in mind one thing: very few people are going to make a million bucks in their first year and go right into retirement.

That said, swing trading can be a very lucrative way to make a living, and if you are interested in business and finance, it can be a lot of fun! In order to get there, you are going to have to study and become an expert in the field. The journey can start with this book. Let's get started!

How Swing Trading Works

It is a style of trading that attempts to catch benefits a securities trading inside one to four days of the period. It is likewise named as a momentary pattern following trading s. Investopedia Explains Swing Trading: To spot circumstances in which a stock or item has super potential to make developments in a shorter period outline, the dealer or the financial specialist must act carefully and quickly. This is predominantly utilized by the home brokers and the informal investors.

Huge foundations for the most part trading measure that are too huge to move all through products quickly. In addition, the merchant or the financial specialist is fit for workaholic behavior the momentary stock developments and that likewise with no challenge with the huge and effective speculators. Swing merchants generally utilize specialized examination to view the stocks and items which are accessible in momentary value motivation.

Such brokers are not intrigued by the crucial estimations of the offers, rather, are keen on realizing the value patterns and different examples.

For what reason is Swing Trading the Preferred Approach? Swing trading is the best proficient methodology towards profiting and money in the entire financial trading. Continuously see the cost from where the stock diagrams start and where it closes.

This is the situation of the customary financial specialist and the merchant. Notwithstanding sitting tight for a really long time periods for any stock or product to move in the normal course, you ought to duplicate your advantages simultaneously and that likewise with both long and short trading s. About $10,000 or more can be earned on the off chance that you trading the all over swings in contrast with the purchasing and holding the stock. In addition, swing trading is superior to anything the day trading in light of the fact that it is compelling than the day trading style, and even the cost related the business set up is additionally low on the grounds that the commissions are not rendered day by day.

The swing dealers likewise have the chance to share among the more critical pieces of the value developments.

Swing Trading May be Right for you if:

If any of the accompanying explanations portray your trading yields,

Swing trading may demonstrate to be directly for you: You are disappointed with the low back up qualities on the purchase and-hold ventures and imagine that there is another better way.

Swing trading will be all the more stuffing for you on the off chance that you won't keep a track on the business sectors entire day. Here and there you may feel dull and depleted, however you should work in a similar issue.

It is certainly for you on the off chance that you have had the option to realize that you can profit just when you will apply your trading s inverse bearings for all your initial trading s of the stocks and wares. What Are Its Benefits The way toward swing trading has turned into a viral stock trading procedure utilized by numerous brokers over the market.

This style of trading has demonstrated to be exceptionally effective for some dedicated stocks and Forex merchants.

Customarily swing trading has been characterized as a progressively theoretical system as the positions are typically purchased and held for the merchant's foreordained time period. These time allotments could go somewhere in the range of two days to a couple of months.

The objective of the swing broker is to recognize the pattern either up or down and place their trading s the most favorable position. From that point, the dealer will ride the heading to what they decide as the depletion point and sell for a benefit.

Regularly, swing brokers will use a wide range of specialized markers that will enable them to have a progressively worthwhile likelihood when making their trading s. Shorter-term brokers don't really will in general swing trading as they incline toward holding positions for the duration of the day and practicing them before the end of the market.

Swing trading methodology uses time, and it is this time is the obstacle factor for a long-time broker. Regularly there is an excessive amount of hazard engaged with the end of the market and that a broker won't acknowledge this hazard. The qualification of swing trading is a wide subject in that it has various impacts from a huge number of various trading procedures. These trading techniques are interesting and have their separate hazard profiles. Swing trading can be a fantastic route for a market member to improve their specialized examination abilities further while enabling them to give more consideration to the crucial side of trading. Numerous fruitful swing merchants have been known to utilize a Bollinger band procedure as a device to help them in entering and leaving positions. Obviously, for a swing broker to be fruitful at the arrangement, they should have a high fitness for deciding the present market pattern and setting their situations by that pattern. It makes a swing merchant note great to put a short post with the arrangement of holding for an all-inclusive period in a market that is drifting upwards. The general subject here is that the objective of the dealers ought to be to build their likelihood of progress while restricting or disposing of hazard. The swing dealer's most noticeably terrible foe is that of a sideways or in a functioning business sector. Sideways value activity will stop a swing broker cold in their tracks as there is no common pattern to key off of.

The Basics Of Swing Trading.

Now, it is time to move on and get to some of the basics about doing an actual swing trade. We are going to take a look at some of the steps that you need to take in order to enter the market, the types of positions that you can choose to take, and even how to take each of the positions that you choose. This will help you to get set up when it is time to do that first trade with this kind of trading strategy!

Choosing to Buy Long or Sell Short

The price of a stock is going to do one of three things at a given time. It will either go down, go up, or it will move sideways. When you enter into the market as a swing trader, you are expecting that the stock is going to either go up or it will go down. If you think that the stock will see an increase in its price, then they will purchase the stock.

This move is going to be considered "going long" or having a "long position" in that stock. For example, if you are long 100 shares of Facebook Inc., it means that you purchased 100 shares of this company and you are making the prediction that you

will be able to sell them at a higher price later on and earn a nice profit.

That one is pretty easy to understand, but what if you are looking at a stock and you expect that the price is going to decrease?

When this situation occurs, you can choose to borrow shares and then later sell them with the expectation that you will purchase them back at a lower price and make a profit later on.

At this point, you may be wondering how it is possible for you to sell shares that you don't own or that you don't hold in your own account?

This is pretty simple. Brokerages have a mechanism that will allow a trader to borrow the shares. When you end up selling shares that you don't actually own, it means that you are "going short" or "being short' on a stock. When a trader says that they are short on a stock, it means that they borrowed shares from the broker and then sold them with the expectations that the price will drop, and they will be able to replace those shares by purchasing them later at a lower price.

When you are setting up an account to trade, you will probably need to take the time to fill out some additional forms with the broker so that you can take this short position with a stock. You should also have an idea that this option can be riskier compared to just going long or purchasing a stock, so you must be actively there to manage the position.

Short selling can be an important tool for you as a swing trader because the prices of the stocks are usually going to drop much faster than they will go up. It is a good rule of thumb to say that stocks are going to fall three times faster than they rise. This is often because of the human psyche; the fear of loss is more powerful than the desire for a gain.

When the stock starts to move down, shareholders are going to fear that they will have to lose their profits or gains, and they move to sell that quickly.

This selling activity is going to feed into more selling as shareholders continue to take the profits and traders start to shorten. This additional shorting activity adds to the downward pressure that is there on the price. This sends the price of the stock into a strong decline, which means that short sellers are able to make a good amount of profits while long traders and other investors are going to enter panic mode and may try to dump their shares to protect themselves.

Knowing this information can make it easier to do the trades that you want. It can help you to figure out which position you would like to enter based on how the market or that particular stock is doing at the time. This also shows you that it is possible to get into the market and make profits, no matter which direction you think the market is heading.

How to Enter a Trade

If you are brand new to trading, you are probably curious about how you would sell or purchase a security. Any time that the market is open, there are going to be two prices for any security that can be traded. There will be the bid price and the ask price. The bid price is what buying or purchasing traders are offering to pay for that stock right then. The ask price, on the other hand, is the price that traders want in order to sell that security.

You will quickly notice that the bid price is always going to be a bit lower simply because the buyers want to pay less, and the asking price is always going to be higher because sellers want more for their holdings.

The difference between these two prices is known as the spread. The spreads that are found will vary for each stock, and they can even change throughout the day. If a stock doesn't have a ton of buyers and sellers, then there could be a bigger spread. When there are more buyers and sellers, then the spread between these two prices will be much lower. As a swing trader, when you are ready to enter into a position, you are going to have two choices. You can either go in or pay the price that the seller is asking for right away or you can place a bid that is at or below the bid price. Paying the asking price immediately can be beneficial because it ensures that the purchase transaction is completed or filled but may mean that you will pay more for it. When a trader places a bit at or below the current bid price, they may be able to make the purchase at a lower price. But, there is the risk that no seller will want to sell for the lower price, and the order may not get filled.

When you are ready to get started with a trade, you will simply need to pick out your trading platform, pick out a stock, and then decide whether you want to pay the asking price or wait and see if you can get it for the bid price. Then, you can enter into the trade and complete the rest of your strategy.

Investment and Margin Accounts

There are two types of accounts that you can choose to open in order to trade stocks. The two main options include the margin account and the investment account. With a margin account, you can borrow against the capital that you have placed in your account. The investment account, on the other hand, will allow you to buy up to the dollar value you hold in that account. You are not able to spend more than what you have put in that account at a time. When you decide to open up a margin account, you may be able to borrow money from the investment or brokerage firm to help pay for some of your investment. This is a process that is known as buying on margin. This can provide you with some advantages of purchasing more shares that you would be able to afford if you just used the capital in your account, and it can help you leverage to get more profits with your money. However, there is a catch with this one in the form of more risks. When you borrow the money to do your investments, there will come a point when you must pay the loan back. If you earn the profits that you think you will, it is easy to pay this back. But, if you lose out and make the wrong predictions, you are going to have to find other ways to pay the money back. Making investments with leverage can magnify the percentage losses on your money.

As a beginner, you should stick with a regular investment account. Trading on margin can increase the amount of risk that you are taking on in your trades.

This may be tempting because it can increase your potential profits, but there is a lot more risk that comes with it as well. You will do much better going with an investment account instead. This way, you can just pull out the money that you are comfortable with rather than hoping that you make a good prediction in the beginning when you are learning.

Picking out a Broker

During this process, we also need to take some time to discuss picking out a broker. If you have already gotten into other forms of trading in the past, then you can simply work with the same broker that you already have. But, if you are getting into trading and this is the first one you have done before, then you will need to search to find the right broker for you. There are many different brokers out there, and many of them can assist you with swing trading. The biggest thing that you will want to look at is the commissions and fees that each broker assesses against you. Since swing trading times are relatively short and you will enter into and out of trades within a few weeks at most with each trade, you want to make sure that the profits you make aren't eaten up by the commissions to your broker. There are different methods that the broker can use to come up with their fees. Some will charge a fixed rate for the whole year. This often works well for long-term trades and probably won't be an option available to you since you will do more trades. The two options that you will most likely deal with include a fee for each trade or a fee based on how much

profit you earn.

If you can, find a broker who will earn a fee based on your profits. This way, you are not charged a ton if you do a bunch of trades during that time. If you earn a good profit, you will have to pay a bit more because of the percentage. If you earn less on one of your trades, then you won't have to pay the broker as much as you did before. Before you enter into any trade, make sure that you discuss the fees with your broker. They should be able to outline their fees and can discuss with you where your money will go when you work with them. This can help you to get a good idea of how much you will spend based on how much you earn, how many trades you decide to enter into, and more. Get the commissions and fees in writing, along with any other agreements that you and the broker and their firm agree to in order to protect you.

Tools And Platforms

Normally, foreign exchange involves selling and purchasing of different currencies across the world.

The number of participants in this market is very large therefore the liquidity is very high. The most unique aspect of the forex trade is that individual traders can compete against large institutions such as hedge funds and commercial banks; all one needs to do is to select the right account and set it up.

There are different types of accounts but the traders have three main options namely mini accounts, standard accounts, and managed accounts. Each account has its own advantages and disadvantages.

The type of account that one opts for depends on factors such as the size of initial capital, risk tolerance levels, and the hours one has to analyze the charts either daily or at different intervals.

Mini Trading Accounts

Simply put, a mini account is one that allows the trader to transact using mini lots. For most brokerage firms, one mini lot equals to 10,000 units.

That is equal to 1/10 of a standard account. Brokerage firms offer mini lots to attract new traders who are still hesitant to trade with bigger accounts or those who do not have the investment funds required.

The advantages of Mini accounts include low risk, low capital required and flexibility. The trader can trade in increments of 10,000 units therefore if he or she is inexperienced, he or she does not have to worry about blowing through their account and capital. Experienced traders can use the mini accounts to test new strategies without excessive risk. A mini account

can be opened with as little as $100, $250 or $500 and the leverage can go up to 400:1. A risk management plan is the key to successful trading and in the case of selecting lots; a trader can minimize the risk by buying a number of mini lots to minimize risk. Remember that one standard lot is equal to about 10 mini lots and diversification reduces risk. The main disadvantage of mini accounts is low reward. A lower risk translates to a lower reward. A mini lot account can only produce $1 per pip movement if it is trading 10000 lots. In a standard account, one pip movement equals to $10.

A subset of the mini account is the micro account which is offered by some online broker. This account has very little risk and also very little reward. The trade is 1000 base currency units and one pip movement earns or loses 10 cents. These accounts are best suited for traders who have very little knowledge about forex trade and one can open using as little as 25 dollars.

Standard Trading Accounts

The standard trading accounts are the most common for traders especially the experienced ones.

These accounts give a trader access to lots of currency worth 100,000 units each. This, however, does not mean that a trader has to put $100,000 in the account as capital so as to trade. The rules of leverage and margin mean that all a trader need is $1000 to have a margin account. The main advantage of this account is the large reward that one might reap with the right strategy and predictions. One pip movement earns $ 10. Again, individuals who own such accounts get better services and perks

because of the upfront capital invested in the account.

The disadvantages include high initial capital and potential for loss. The kind of capital required to set up a standard account can deter many traders from venturing in it. Again, the higher the risk, the higher the returns and the vice versa holds, A standard account trader has a higher risk of loss because if a lot falls with 100 pips, he or she loses $1000. Such loses can be devastating for beginner traders.

Managed Trading Accounts

Managed accounts are accounts where one puts in the capital but does not make the decisions to sell or buy. Such accounts are handled by account managers such as stockbrokers and stock managers. In this case, the traders set objectives for the managers (the expected returns, risk management) and the managers have to meet them.

Managed accounts are categorized into two major types namely Pooled funds and Individual accounts. In pooled funds, the money of different investors is put into an investment vehicle referred to as mutual fund and the profits generated are shared. The accounts are further classified by risk tolerance. If a trader is looking for higher returns, he or she may put his money in a high risk/reward account while those looking for long term steady income can invest in lower risk accounts. Under managed accounts, the individual accounts are managed by a broker each in its own capacity, unlike the pooled funds where the manager uses all the money together.

The main advantage of managed accounts is that one gets professional advice and guidance. An experienced professional forex account manager will be making the decisions and this is a benefit that one can use. Again, a trader gets to trade without having to spend hours analyzing the charts and watching for developments.

One disadvantage that deters traders from venturing into this account is the high price. One should be aware that the majority of managed accounts require one to put in at least $2000 in the pooled account and $10000 for the individual accounts. To add to this cost, the managers are entitled to a commission which is calculated monthly or yearly. The managed accounts are also very inflexible for the trader. If he or she sees an opportunity to trade, he or she will not be able to make a move but will rely on the manager to decide.

Note

It is advisable for a swing trader to use the demo accounts offered by brokers before investing in real money regardless of the account he or she opts to use. Demo accounts allow one to practice without risk and also to try out different strategies. One rule that every trader should apply is to never invest in a real account unless they are completely satisfied with it. One of the main differences between success and failure in forex exchange is the account selected.

Opening an Account

Forex exchange has been around for very many years and some say that it is as old as the invention of national currencies.

Over the years, the market has grown so much so that it is the biggest market across the world. However, it has not been accessible to the public as easily as it is today.

From the 1990s when the era of the internet begun, many retail forex brokers have established routes through which anyone can trade in currencies so long as they can access the internet and have some money.

There is a lot of hype and information about forex trade on the internet but not everybody understands how to select and open an account.

Currently, opening a forex account has become as easy as opening a bank account or another type of brokerage account.

Some of the typical requirements are a name, phone number, address, email, a password, account currency type, country of citizenship, date of birth, employment status, and tax id or Social security number. Opening an account may also require one to answer some financial questions such as their net worth, annual income, trading objectives, and trading experience. Before one starts to trade on the foreign exchange market, they should make some considerations to ensure that they have a positive, secure and successful experience.

The Right Broker

The first step to trading well is to find the right broker. The activities of forex exchange are decentralized and there are hardly any regulations.

Because of the over the counter nature, traders are advised to identify a reliable broker. This involves conducting researches on the reputation of the broker; to identify if there is a history of irregular practices.

One may also want to comprehensively understand the services offered by the particular broker before setting up an account. While some brokerages support basic and plain vanilla activities, others offer very sophisticated trading platforms. Some brokers will offer the trader analytical resources to support better decision making while others won't.

Again, a trader should assess the fees and commissions for different brokers. Majority of Brokers charge some fees for their services through the bid-ask spread and in many cases, it is not a large percentage. However, some brokerages have some other fees and commissions and they might be hidden from the trader. When one is considering the extra costs, he or she should check if it is worthwhile.

The Procedure

Opening a foreign exchange account is not hard but traders should have a few things to get started. The trader will have to provide some identification information such as name, phone number, country of origin et cetera. Besides, the trader will be required to state his or her trade intentions and their level of knowledge and experience in the trade. The steps of opening an account may vary depending on the brokerage firm but normally it involves:

- Accessing the website of the broker and study the accounts available. The accounts include small ones where the trader can trade with minimum capital such as mini accounts or the sophisticated accounts designed for experienced traders such as standard trading account.

- Completing an application form,

- Getting registered (user name and password) to access the account.

- Log in to the client portal and arrange for a transfer of money from the bank to the forex account. These deposits can be done through credit or debit card, checks, or electronic transfers.

- Once the funds are transferred, the trader is ready to start trading. Before trading, the trader may review the recommendations made by the brokers or extra services offered such as simulator programs.

Online Trading

It refers to buying and selling stocks or other assets by the use of a broker's internet-based website or trading platform. Currencies, futures, options, ETFs, mutual funds, bonds, and stocks can all be traded online. It is called self-directed investing or e-trading. As mentioned above, in a split of a second you can trade stocks and other financial instruments such as the Dollar or Euro, some commodities such as Gold or Oil as well as main market indices.

One more advantage of online trading is that the improvement in the rate of which trades can be implemented and settled, since there is no demand for paper-based files to be reproduced, registered and entered into a digital format.

Once an investor opens a buy position on the internet, the trade is set in a database that assesses for the very best price by searching all of the marketplace trades that trade the inventory in the investor's currency.

The market with the very best price fits the buyer with a vendor and sends the confirmation to the purchaser's agent and the seller's agent. All this process can be achieved within minutes of opening a trade, in comparison to making a telephone call that requires several confirmation steps before the representative can input the purchase.

It is all up to investors or stock traders to do their research about a broker before opening trading accounts with the business. Before an account is opened, the customer will be requested to complete a questionnaire about their investment and financial history to ascertain which sort of trading accounts is acceptable for the customer.

On the flip side, an experienced trader who would love to execute various trading strategies will be provided with a margin account where he can purchase, brief, and compose securities such as shares, options, futures, and currencies. Not all securities are all readily available to be traded on the internet, depending upon your broker. Some agents need you to call them to put a transaction on any shares trading on the pink sheets and choose stocks trading over-the-counter.

Additionally, not all agents ease derivatives trading in currencies and commodities throughout their affiliate platforms. Because of this, it is necessary that the dealer knows what a broker offers before registering with the trading platform.

Most online trading classes are centered on instructing marketplace mechanisms and technical evaluation, while others might concentrate on more specific strategies or particular asset classes. Courses may offer a comprehensive summary of technical analysis in addition to other strategies designed for specific asset classes. They assist traders quickly reach a stage where they are comfortable creating approaches and executing trades.

Fundamental analysis.

Of the two most broadly perceived swing trading styles, swing exchanging and utilizing a purchase to hold venture system, swing exchanging is by a long shot the most appropriate style for alternatives. The purchase to hold procedure is not generally reasonable by any means, since choices are essentially momentary exchanging instruments. Most contracts lapse following a couple of months or shorter, and even the more extended term leaps typically terminate following one year. Accordingly, alternatives are the ideal device for swing exchanging. Swing trading is much less exceptional than day exchanging and furthermore significantly less tedious. With day exchanging, you must be set up to spend the entire day checking the business sectors while trusting that the ideal time will enter and leave positions. The degrees of focus required can be extremely depleting, and it requires an unmistakable range of abilities to be fruitful utilizing this style. Swing exchanging, then again, is an ideal center ground for those that need to see a sensibly brisk profit for their cash yet do not have room schedule-wise to devote to purchasing and sell throughout the day, consistently.

It's an incredible style for those that are relative amateurs and those that hold down all day occupations or have other time responsibilities during the working day. It's conceivable to feature potential swings, enter the important position, and afterward simply check how your position is faring toward the finish of every day, or even every couple of days, before choosing whether or not to leave that position. The nuts and bolts of this style are generally simple to get to grasps with, which is another valid justification for giving it a go. You do not have a colossal measure of information to begin with; you simply need to know how choices work and be set up to devote a sensible measure of time to searching for the correct chances. There are definitely dangers included, however this style to a great extent empowers you to go out on a limb that you are alright with despite everything it allows you to make some better than average benefits. You can set stop misfortunes or use spreads so you are never in peril of losing more cash than you are alright with. You can really utilize spreads in an assortment of systems, some of which are especially valuable for swing exchanging when you are not for all time checking value changes in the market. **Guidance for Swing Trading Options**

Arranging and investigating are significant for anybody hoping to utilize this style.

You ought to be solid and steady and have a smart thought of precisely what sorts of examples and patterns you are searching for and what kind of exchanges you are going to make in some random circumstance.

You do need there to be a sure measure of adaptability in the manner you exchange, yet it can have an unmistakable arrangement of targets and a characterized arrangement

for how you will accomplish those objectives. The market can be eccentric so you should probably change in like manner. Anyway a strong arrangement in any event gives you a stage to work from.

It is a smart thought to set most extreme misfortunes on any position that you enter.

It's improbable that you will get your expectations and conjectures right every time you enter a position, and some of the time the costs will move against you.

You ought to dependably be set up to cut your misfortunes and escape a terrible position; it can and will occur and you simply need to ensure that your great exchanges exceed your awful exchanges. Great expository abilities are valuable.

You don't need to settle on choices as fast as though you were day exchanging so you have room schedule-wise to investigate circumstances and work out the best passage and leave purposes of a specific example or pattern that you distinguish.

It's likewise imperative to be persistent. In the event that you can't locate a decent section point to exploit a value swing, at that point you need the control and tolerance to hold up until an open door presents itself.

You don't should make exchanges each day if there are no reasonable ones to be made, and the way to progress is extremely about picking the correct chances and executing your exchanges at the opportune time. Correspondingly, you ought to dependably have an objective benefit for a position, and close your position when you have made that benefit. Attempting to press additional benefit out of a vacant position can simply bring about losing your benefits. You can undoubtedly set your parameters for constraining misfortunes and securing benefits by utilizing stop orders, alternatives spreads, or a mix of the both.

Alternatives Brokers for Swing Trading Options

A standout amongst the most significant choices you have to make before beginning with this, or some other style, is which stock merchant would it be advisable for you to utilize? Utilizing an online intermediary is not as fundamental for swing exchanging for what it's worth for day exchanging, yet you could utilize a customary representative in the event that you needed. Be that as it may, there are as yet numerous points of interest to utilizing an online merchant; for instance they by and large offer less expensive charges and commissions which will enable you to put in your requests.

Financial Instruments For Swing

Whether you know it or not, you're already ahead of almost all the novice traders out there and most of the unsuccessful traders as well.

The idea of taking the order flow into account when determining your strategy is not something you will read about too much so take the time to really study this well. It will be alien at first, especially if you've read other books which promise magical indicators, but you will reap the rewards of your effort.

When determining their strategy in the markets, most traders make the mistake of sticking to one method and try to fit it to multiple market environments (or landscapes).

This is an absurd thing to do. Would you wear just swimming trunks when the weather outside is below zero? Would you bundle up in 4 layers when it's 100 degrees outside? Yet again, we see how common sense gets thrown out of the window for some reason when it comes to trading.

Everything comes down to (if you're following along, you know what's coming next) order flow.

Order Flow and Your Strategies

The order flow determines the charting landscape and the landscape determines your strategy. It really is that simple. It doesn't matter which indicator you use, which magical formula or mathematical regression tactic, it all comes down to which phase or what type of order flow is currently present.

This is what makes it possible to make money using a simple moving average strategy (we'll explain this later) as well as with a far more complicated indicator. Indicators which are meant to indicate trend direction and characteristics of a trend must be used in trending environments. Indicators which oscillate between extremes must be used in a ranging environment.

Easy to Understand, Tough to Follow

It's easy enough to say 'use this in a trend' and 'use this in a range'. Technically you can get away with just two indicators right? Well, right! However, the key point is identifying what is a trending environment and what is a range.

You see, markets rarely move in a uniform fashion. You will see trends with big counter-trend participation, ranges which move in a channel and at a slight angle, etc. It's very rare to see a strong, explosive move which sustains itself over long period of time or to see a clean range with the upper and lower boundaries being cleanly respected.

So what's the solution? Well, you can't change the market's behavior. Hence, you need to modulate and determine what your behavior is going to be, given the market environment. If you're unable to determine what's going on, as previously mentioned, simply step aside and wait. When you're a novice, the best things you can do for your own sake is to wait and watch. Unfortunately, most novices do the exact opposite and rush to trade. A good idea is to perhaps develop some sort of graded scale to help you determine the strength of the trend. The stronger the trend, the lesser the number of counter-trend traders. The weaker the trend, the greater the number of counter-trend traders.

A range would of course be the weakest possible trend present in the markets given that it has equally balanced order distribution.

You could decide to trade only the strongest trends and the most obvious ranges; in other words, both extremes of the graded scale you develop. Over time, as your skill grows, you expand to cover more scenarios and thus build your confidence. As mentioned before, there is no magic pill here you can take. The only way forward is via persistent hard work.

A Simple Execution Checklist

In lieu of the above, it would be best for you to develop an execution checklist. It could be as follows:

- Is price in a trend or range? Or can't say?

- How strong is the trend (if in a trend)? How defined/clean is the range (if in a range)? Assign a number on the scale if using one.

- Is this number something I'm comfortable with to participate further?

- If so, what are my trend strategies (if in a trend)? What are my range strategies (if in a range)?

- Execute.

Again, this is easy to write down but difficult to execute because of the highly charged trading environment newbies partake in. The mental aspect of trading is an important skill you must master if you are to succeed. For now, just remember what was said earlier about the ideal trading state being one of slightly bored attachment. If you are not in this state, then do not trade.

When to and When Not to

At this point, it would serve us well to list out a few do's and don'ts of trading.

Do not trade if:

- Your state is one of over excitement or action seeking.

- Your state is depressed, sad or overwhelmed.

- You feel hurried or rushed and feel like there's too much going on and can't keep up.

- You want to make money in a hurry and NOW!

- You think you've found the ultimate strategy which unlocks all market secrets.

- You're dreaming of luxury cars and mansions and total financial independence.

Do trade if:

- You recognize how much more you need to learn and are determined to put in the work.

- You know you are willing and ready to step aside and admit "I don't know."

- You are risking only what you can afford to lose as capital.

- You are realistic about your money goals. The world's biggest hedge funds consider a 15% annual return a brilliant performance. You're OK with producing this much amount of money from your trading.

This chapter has strayed a bit beyond the technical aspects of trading and into the mindset and risk portion of your trading skills. For now, you must understand that your trading success depends on much more than just your technical strategy. You need to master risk management as well as your mindset.

Ideally, you will start working on your mindset first, then your risk management and then finally on your technical strategy. With most people though, this is reversed. This is OK as long as you work on all aspects and not just the technical portion, expecting some secret to be unlocked via some unknown indicator. You might as well learn now that no such thing exists. Never has and never will.

Successful traders make money via mastery in all three aspects of trading: Technical Skills, Mindset and Risk Management. It behooves you to master all aspects of all three.

Now with that little warning, it is time to delve into the individual indicators and strategies you can use with them as part of your technical plan to trade. They're great tools but they need to be used appropriately. No one ever built a cabinet using a hammer to drive screws after all.

When it comes to trading on the stock market, financial instruments are the specific asset that you are trading each time you buy and sell new stocks. Financial instruments represent stocks, bonds, commodities, currencies, and any other valuable instrument that can be traded within a company. From the market perspective, there are five major financial instruments that you can trade: exchange-traded funds (ETFs), individual stocks, currencies, crypto-currencies, and options. We are going to discuss what each of these are in this chapter, and which you should consider trading as a beginner.

Even if you are only planning on becoming involved in one particular financial instrument, such as ETFs or options, it is important that you educate yourself on what the other forms of financial instruments are.

This way, if and when you are ready to diversify your portfolio, you have a strong idea of what else you can get into trading and how it works.

Furthermore, as you read through blogs and various news articles to keep up to date on the market, you are going to see these terms being used in plenty of scenarios. Knowing what you are reading about can help you educate yourself, further improving your ability to make educated decisions on your own trades.

Exchange-Traded Funds (ETFs)

Exchange-traded funds, or ETFs, are the most popular financial instrument to be traded amongst beginners.

When you trade an ETF, rather than trading something specific such as an individual stock or a commodity, you are trading more of a financial basket which keeps several different financial instruments in it. Most ETFs are made up of individual stocks, commodities, bonds, or even a mixture of these particular financial instruments.

The "basket" or ETF is then awarded an associated price that can easily be bought and sold. As the ETF is bought and sold, the price fluctuates, which means that ETF prices fluctuate more than virtually any other financial instrument on the market.

Some ETFs are US only, whereas others can be traded internationally.

Before you get involved in buying and selling stocks with ETFs it is a good idea to do your research and get an idea of where yours can be bought and sold, as this will help you educate yourself on whether or not it is worth your investment.

Regarding ETFs, their fees are often quite a bit lower than any other financial instrument that you can trade.

The commissions paid to your brokerage are going to be significantly lower than they would be if you bought each stock individually, which means that you are actually going to end up with more money in your pocket at the end of the day, too. I strongly recommend that when you start out with swing trading you start out with ETFs, as they are going to be the easiest for you to understand. This way, too, rather than having to research and follow various different individual stocks, you can simply follow one ETF.

Although ETFs are simple and continue to be the best trades that you can make, it is important to understand that there are some drawbacks to trading in them. One of the biggest drawbacks is that people tend to become complacent and trade exclusively in one form of stock or another, and never fully diversify their portfolio. In certain ETFs this is not necessarily so bad because the fund itself is diversified, but if you trade in something more specific such as commodities, this can massively reduce your diversification. As well, if you do choose to have your ETFs actively managed by a brokerage, it can cost more, so it is truly best to learn how to do it yourself. Spending money on a brokerage will only cut into your earnings unnecessarily.

Individual Stocks

When people get started investing in the stock market, what they often expect they are going to be investing in are individual stocks. Investing in individual stocks is not ideal for beginners because they are harder to track and their patterns are more volatile and less predictable than other stocks. With individual stocks, you really need to be able to gauge the likely success or growth of a company to be able to predict whether or not the valuation of your stocks is going to improve enough over time to make the trade worth it.

Many times, when individual people get invested in individual stocks they are doing so to diversify their portfolio, as well as to take the gamble at earning more from their investments. That is because, as with anything, the higher risk of individual stocks can also lead to a higher reward from stocks.

If you do decide to get involved in individual stocks, you should be prepared to pay higher brokerage fees, or to have to engage in far more trades on your own.

You should also be prepared to follow the market much more closely as you are going to need to know exactly what is going on in your particular stock, so that you can buy and sell at the right times.

If you are not following the market closely, you could find yourself missing out on massive amounts of profits in a relatively short amount of time.

As a result, you can completely destroy your ability to earn any significant income from this particular trade method. Beyond the additional fees and market research you are going to have to do, buying and selling individual stocks also requires a high amount of personal discipline as you are going to need to be able to avoid making emotional decisions in your trades. For many people, it can be challenging to hold on when the market drops greatly, as you may have an intense fear that it will never come back up for that particular stock. As a result, you could drastically short yourself on earnings due to emotional decisions, when in reality what you should have been doing was holding on and waiting for the market to balance out again. Unless you have a strong sense of personal discipline, a clear understanding of the market, experience with trading, and the willingness to invest more time and money into your trades, you should refrain from using individual stocks. These are better reserved for people who have already invested a healthy amount into other stocks, such as ETFs, and who are interested in playing around and taking larger risks with a smaller amount of their investable funds. This way, you are not at risk of losing everything due to a poor investment choice.

Trading Currencies

When it comes to trading currencies: it is exactly what you would expect. You buy currency and sell it. Trading currencies is actually largely what places a certain numerical value on each currency, and is directly responsible for the strengths and weaknesses in the values of different currencies.

Typically, currencies that are commonly traded are worth far more, whereas those that are not traded nearly as often are not worth quite as much. When it comes to trading currencies, the market is open 24 hours a day from Monday morning to Friday evening. They close for the weekends, but are otherwise open nonstop. A person that trades currencies trades in what is known as "lots," which suggests the amount or lot of currency that you are trading. 1,000 is a lot of $1,000 in the base currency, and is known as a "micro lot." Mini lots are 10,000 or $10,000 or your base currency, and standard lots are 100,000 or $100,000 of your base currency. Unlike individual stocks, where you can buy and sell just one single stock, you trade currencies in what is known as pairs, meaning that you buy one currency and then sell another. If you choose to trade in currency, there are 18 commonly traded currencies that can be paired together to create your trades. While many other currencies exist, they are not traded on the market, which means that you cannot buy and sell them. Of the 18 currencies that you can buy and trade on the market, only 8 of them are incredibly popular to trade. Those 8 currencies include: the Canadian Dollar (CAD), the U.S. Dollar (USD), the British Pound (GBP), the Euro (EUR), the New Zealand Dollar (NZD), the Swiss Franc (CHF), the Japanese Yen (JPY), and the

Australian Dollar (AUD). Although you can certainly trade with the other 10, most trades happen exclusively in these currencies, and you should stick with them too if you are going to get into currency trading.

Risk And Account Management

Risk management is a deliberate action taken by a trader or investor. The purpose is to keep losses at a minimum. As a trader, you are exposed to a lot of dangers. You can lose money if you are not careful or if your strategy was not successful. Should you lose money in a trade, then the risk can be managed. All that you need to do is to open yourself up to being profitable in the market.

Risk management is a grossly neglected area of every unsuccessful trader's strategy. Indeed, most do not even understand the concept and fail to explore it beyond the cursory nod given to stop losses and per trade risk.

Perfect risk management can save a poor strategy but even the best strategy cannot save poor risk management. Many of you must have heard of this piece of wisdom but probably very few of you truly understand its implications.

Risk in trading is quite simple. It is the probability of you losing your capital on a series of trades, including the current one.

Plan Your Trades

Some of the best tools you will need as part of your risk management plan are take-profit and stop-loss. Using these two tools, you can plan your trades in advance. You will need to use technical analysis in order to determine these two points. With this information, you should be able to determine the price you are willing to pay as well as the losses you can incur.

Adhere to a Proven Trading Method

Furthermore, do not transform it. In the event that you have a demonstrated technique however it does not appear to work in a given exchanging session, do not return home that night and attempt to devise another. In the event that your strategy works for more than one-portion of the exchanging sessions, at that point stay with it. Keep in mind, the Holy Grail of exchanging is cashing the executives.

Consistency is Confidence

How great does it feel have the option to turn on your exchanging stage the morning realizing that, on the off chance that you play by the guidelines, the likelihood of fruitful exchanging day is generally high? The appropriate response? Great! Keep in mind: If you make somewhat consistently, at that point you have earned the privilege to exchange greater.

Try not to Chase the Markets

Proficient merchants that pick Admiral Markets will be satisfied to realize that they can exchange totally chance free with a FREE demo exchanging account. Rather than going to the live markets and putting your capital in danger, you can dodge the hazard out and out and essentially practice until you are prepared to change to live exchanging.

Pursue Your Trading Routine

Never attempt to break your exchanging schedule. Pursue real markets and exchange just during the significant markets. These include: New York, London and Tokyo markets. The value moves all the more detectably during significant market sessions, so you can disregard minor markets. Significant markets furnish you with an incredible number of arrangements as well.

Maintaining a trading Journal

You can do this online or keep a paper copy nearby. When you are done with one trade, make sure to write down what happened during that trade, what strategy you used, what was going on in the market, how much you spent, and more. If you ever get stuck with one of your trades or you aren't sure how to handle one situation or another, you can refer back to this journal and see what advice it has.

You may be surprised that, after a particularly hard situation in a different trade, you can look back in this journal and find the answers that you need.

More than anything else, your trade journal is what will keep your risk management on track. Your journal should, at a minimum, record your trade date, instrument, direction (long or short), stop loss size, reasons for entering, exit date, P/L and any comments.

As a trader, you need to keep a journal so that you have a reliable record of your trades and their performance. This is one of the best ways of learning about your style and performance. Trade tracking journals also enables you to track your trades and the actions you took during certain situations and instances.

In short, a trading journal provides traders with the necessary tools and information that they need to evaluate their trading activities objectively.

As a trader, you really should be tracking your trades throughout the day. A journal helps you to keep a record of the happenings each day as well as your reactions or actions. Your plan should include a tried and tested system that suits your trading style. Make sure that you test this system and review it often then improve your trading plans and performance.

Setting Target and Stops

We can define a stop-loss as the total amount of loss that a trader is willing to incur in a single trade. Beyond the stop-loss point, the trader exits the trade. This is basically meant to prevent further losses by thinking the trade will eventually get some momentum.

We also have what is known as a take-profit point. It is at this point that you will collect any profits made and possibly exit a trade. At this point, a particular stock or other security is often very close to the point of resistance.

Beyond this point, a reversal in price is likely to take place. Rather than lose money, you should exit the trade. Traders sometimes take profit and let a particular trade continue if it was still making money. Another take-profit point is then plotted. If you have a good run, you are allowed to lock in the profits and let the good run continue.

Assessing Risk versus Reward

A lot of traders tend to think of the outcome of their trade in terms of the amount they make, that is, $100 or -$50 and so on. This is a warped way of thinking since it places an undue amount of importance on the amount of money one makes.

This is not to say it's unimportant but the best way to make money trading isn't in following this method. Instead, you need to measure the outcome of your trades as a function of your risk per trade, that is, as a multiple of your R (R being the percent of your capital you risk per trade).

Thus on a loss, your profit/loss record (P/L) will read -R and on a win your P/L will read 1.5R or 2R and so on. Recording it this way puts the focus squarely on your risk management and forces you to think in terms of risk.

A lot of traders lose a lot of money at the markets for a very simple reason.

They do not know about risk management or how to go about it. This mostly happens to beginners or novice traders. Most of them simply learn how to trade then rush to the markets in the hope of making a kill. Sadly, this is now how things work because account and risk management are not taken into consideration. Think about it this way. Supposing someone you don't trust many approaches you for a $1,000 loan with a promise to pay you back with $100 interest after a month. You may be hesitant because the risk is greater compared than the profit. However, if he promises to pay you back after one month with a $2,000 interest, then the risk is well worth it. The ratio of risk versus reward, in this case, is 2:1. A lot of investors believe this to be an excellent ratio and many would take it because they get a chance to double their money.

If the borrower offered to pay back $3,000, then the risk vs. reward ratio increases to 3:1.

A trader who is unsuccessful will likely look at an entry and then only think about the profit they will make on that trade. But, a trader who is successful is always going to consider the upside and the downside with any trade they choose. So, they are going to think about how much of a risk they are going to have if they take a loss. It is all about comparing the amount of risk that you are going to take to the reward that you are hoping to get from that trade.

For the reward, they are hoping that the XBI stock is going to reach $91.00 for each share or the prior area of resistance. This can help them earn $3.50 a share for this one. This means that, in this scenario, the risk is $1.00 a share, but the reward is a potential $3.50 a share. This ends up being a very good risk to reward ratio. If the reward only ended up being $0.75 a share, then it is best to look for another option since the risk is too high for that trade.

Always ensure to apply the risk versus reward ratio for all your trades. Keep in mind the indicated acceptable levels. If you are unable to find acceptable ratios after trying several times, find another security. Once you learn how to incorporate risk management into your trades, you will become safer as you trade without incurring any huge losses.

Managing the Trade Size

As a trader, you also need to make determinations regarding other aspects of the trade. These include the number of stock or currency or any other financial markets' instruments. When doing this, most traders overlook position size. They feel like it is not important enough or sometimes they have no clue that it is necessary and how to determine an optimum one.

Some traders have large accounts and wish they could spend freely. These usually employ different approaches when it comes to position size.

Even if you had an account worth $500,000, then you would not want to risk over $500 per trade. This is equivalent to 1% of the total amount in the account.

Sometimes, people choose stop levels for the day. These are daily stop orders issued by a client to their broker and so on. Daily stop-loss points simply indicate the amount of money that you are ready to lose per trade. Should this level be attained as you trade, then you will have to stop trading and exit all other possible positions in the market.

Experienced traders usually opt to equate the daily stop-loss positions as equivalent to their average profitability. So if a person makes $400, then their stop loss order will be a lot closer to this figure.

Keep Your Emotions in Check

Keeping your emotions in check is especially important when you find a stock going against you. Not only does this make you realize that you made a mistake during your analysis and any calculations, which carries its own emotions, but this can also make you go through a series of emotional stages. There are many traders and investors who state that this series of five stages is similar to the five stages of grief.

Follow the 1% Rule

One of the biggest ways to reduce your risk is to make sure that you focus on keeping your proportion low. One of the best ways to do this is to only risk about 1% of the money in your account with each trade. For example, if you have $10,000 in your account, this means that you will not trade more than $100 on a trade.

However, many expert swing traders believe that when you are first starting out, you should lower this even more. Therefore, a beginner should look at trading no more than around 0.3% to 0.5%. While this doesn't seem like a lot of money, most stocks generally aren't a large amount of money to buy. Some of the most expensive stocks to buy will be blue-chip stocks.

Determine a Stop-Loss Amount

After you have looked at setting your risk at 1%, you can look at another factor, which is setting your trade risk. This is when you set your stop-loss amount. This amount will be created when you set up your trading plan. For example, if you spent $10.00 on your trade, then you might set up your stop-loss level at $9.80.

This means that once you reach this amount, you will sell that stock and only lose .20 cents. Most traders will look at the percentage of their account they put towards their stock in order to help them determine their stop-loss amount. This is because some traders might feel more comfortable setting their stop-loss amount at a higher percentage if they followed the 1% rule than an if they decided to go up to 3% or even 5%.

Follow Your Guidelines and Rules

As you get started in your trading career, you will start to develop your own rules and guidelines, such as in your trading plan. It is important that you don't change any of these rules and guidelines without fully looking at your trade as a whole. On top of this, it is important to follow because it will help keep you focused, you will begin to learn the details of swing trading easier as you won't be so concerned about your next step, and you will feel more comfortable in your abilities.

Fundamental Analysis

Fundamental analysis can be described as a method of evaluating securities such as stocks.

The aim is to measure the intrinsic value of a company or its stock. We carry out fundamental analysis by closely examining financial reports, economic prospects, as well as other quantitative and qualitative factors. Basically, you study anything that pertains to the value of the company's security.

There are plenty of professionals who conduct stock and company analysis.

They include traders such as stock traders, stock analysts, fund managers, and many others. As a swing trader, you need to learn how to carry out a thorough fundamental analysis of any stock or security that you are interested in.

Fundamental analysis is the backbone of any investment process. You can only be regarded as a successful trader or investor if you can successfully perform fundamental analysis.

When we talk of fundamentals, we actually mean the quantitative and qualitative data that significantly contributes to the success and financial valuation of a company. It also includes an assessment of both macroeconomics and microeconomics aspects. These are aspects that are essential for determining the worth of a company or other assets.

Microeconomics and Macroeconomics

Macroeconomics stands for all factors that affect the general economy. These are factors such as inflation, supply and demand, unemployment and even GDP growth. They also include international trade and prevailing monetary and fiscal policies put forth by the authorities. Macroeconomic considerations are useful when it comes to matters of large-scale analysis of the economy and how these relate to business activities.

Microeconomic factors are those that focus on the smaller elements of the economy. These include elements in certain particular sectors of a market. For example, labor issues in a given market, matters such as supply and demand and others such as labor and consumer issues relating to the said industry.

An Example One of the world's most successful stock analysts and traders is Warren Buffet. He uses fundamental analysis to determine which shares to buy and which companies to invest in. His success as an analyst has turned him into a billionaire. Apart from analyzing companies, the equities market can also be analyzed. There are some analysts who conducted a fundamental analysis of the S&P 500 for a period of a week. This was from 4th July to 8th July 2016. Within this period of time, the S&P index went up to 2129.90 following the release of an impressive jobs report within the US. This was an unprecedented performance surpassed only by the May 2015 which was 2132.80. The superb performance was attributed to the announcement of 287,000 new jobs across the country.

Intrigues of Fundamental Analysis

Some of the parameters that analysts look at within a company's financial statement include a measure of solvency, profitability, liquidity, growth trajectory, efficiency, and leverage. Analysts also use rations to work out the financial health of companies. Examples of such ratios include quick ratio and current ratio. These rations are useful in determining a company's ability to repay short-term liabilities based on their current assets.

To find the current ratio, you will divide the current assets with the current liabilities. These figures can easily be accessed from the company's balance sheet. While there is no ratio that is considered ideal, anything below 1 is considered a poor financial situation that is incapable of meeting all short-term debts.

The balance sheet also provides analysts with additional information such as current debt amounts owed by the company. In such a situation, then the analysis will focus on the debt ratio. This is computed by working out all the liabilities and dividing by the total assets. When the ratio is computed, a ratio greater than 1 points to a company with a lot more debt compared to its assets. This means that should interest rates rise, then the firm may default on its debts.

Stock Analysis

Stock analysis can be defined as the process used by traders and investors to acquire in-depth information about stock or company. The analysis is done by evaluating and studying current and past data about the stock or even company. This way, traders and investors are able to gain a significant edge in the market as they will be in a position to make well-informed decisions.

The stock analysis involves not just current financial reports but also compares the current financial statements with those from previous years. This will give a trader or investor a feel of the company's performance and will determine whether the firm is stable, receding, or growing. It is also common for an analyst to compare a company's financial statement with those of other companies in the same sector. This is done in order to compare profitability and other parameters.

Of great importance is the operating profit. It is a measure of the revenue that a company is left with after other expenses have been cleared. Basically, a firm with operating margins of 0.27 is viewed favorably when compared with one whose margin is 0.027, for instance. This can be translated to mean that the firm whose operating margin is 0.27 spends 73 cents per dollar earned to foot its operating costs.

Benefits of Undertaking Fundamental Analysis

There are lots of benefits of conducting a thorough fundamental analysis of a company. Here is a look at some of these benefits.

1. Long-term Trends

Fundamental analysis is excellent for investors and traders, especially long-term investors. Patient investors looking to invest in the long term as well as traders seeking solid, reliable companies will definitely benefit from the analysis.

2. Identification of Valuable Companies

The reliable fundamental analysis enables investors and traders to identify firms that are of high value and worth investing in. A lot of notable investors always look for valuable companies. They include John Neff and Warren Buffet. Valuable companies will have a strong balance sheet, staying power, stable earnings, and valuable assets.

3. Business Acumen

Fundamental analysis will help you develop a deep understanding of the business. For instance, you will become familiar with profit drivers and revenue sources of the company. For instance, earning expectations and actual earnings are extremely useful when it comes to equity and stock prices.

Technical Analysis

This is another method used by analysts, investors, and traders to analyze stocks and companies. This type of analysis pays closer attention to previous market action and how this can be used to predict future performance. In this instance, an analyst, or trader, will analyze the entire market and will focus their attention on volume and price. Other factors looked at include supply and demand as well as any

essential factors that can move the market.

One of the most crucial tools for technical analysis is a chart. Charts are key for successful analysis of any market or particular stocks or companies. They provide a graphical presentation of stock and its trend within a given time period. For instance, a technical analyst can use a chart to indicate some areas as either resistance or support levels.

Resistance levels are placed above a stock's prevailing market price while support levels are indicated by previous lows that occur just below the current or prevailing market price. Should there be a break below support levels is a pointer to a bearish trend in the market. On the other hand, any break that occurs just above resistance levels will point to a bullish outlook.

Factors that Direct Technical Analysis

Technical analysis outcomes are only effective if the analysis of the price trend is affected by demand and supply forces. However, when other external factors come into play and affect price movement, then technical analysis of the stock may not be successful. For instance, stock prices can be affected by factors such as dividend announcements, the exit or death of company CEO, mergers, stock splits, change of management, monetary policy, and so on. It is common for analysts to conduct both technical and fundamental analysis together even though they can be conducted separately. Some choose to apply only one while others prefer both methods for stock and company analysis.

In order to come up with a successful investment strategy for your portfolio, then you will need to do some analysis and vet market sectors, stocks, and the markets.

Technical analysis is simply the process of forecasting the future movement of stocks on the markets according to past stock price movements. Just like weather predictions, technical analysis does not produce 100% accurate results.

However, technical analysis provides traders, and investors, with information which they can use to anticipate the price movement over time. There is a wide variety of charts that are used to help determine the future price movements of a particular stock.

Details of Technical Analysis

Technical analysis can be applied to numerous securities including Forex, stocks, futures, commodities, indices, and many more. The price of a security depends on a collection of metrics. These are volume, low, open, high, close, open interest, and so on. These are also known as market action or price data.

There are a couple of assumptions that we make as traders when performing technical analysis. However, remember that it is applicable only in situations where the price is only a factor of demand and supply. If there are other factors that can influence prices significantly, then the technical analysis will not work. The following assumptions are often made about securities that are being analyzed.

There are no Artificial Price Movements:

Artificial price movements are usually as a result of distributions, dividends, and splits. Such changes in stock price can greatly alter the price chart and this tends to cause technical analysis to be very difficult to implement. Fortunately, it is possible to remedy this. All that you need to do as an analyst is to make adjustments to historic data before the price changes.

The Stock is Highly Liquid:

Another major assumption that technical analysis makes is that the stock is highly liquid. Liquidity is absolutely crucial for volumes. When stocks are heavily traded as a result of liquidity and volume, then traders are able to easily enter and exit trades. Stocks that are not highly traded tend to be rather difficult to trade because there are very few sellers and buyers at any point in time. Also, stocks with low liquidity are usually poorly priced, sometimes at less than a penny for each share. This is risky as they can be manipulated by investors.

Study the Charts

Experts always advise traders to closely examine the chart of the stock they intend to buy as part of the technical analysis. When you examine the charts, you will be looking to spot the bottom and identify the best entry points. You will also examine the ceiling in order to identify the ideal exit points. All investors purchase stocks hoping the price will almost immediately go up. It is, therefore, crucial to look at and understand historic chart patterns of the particular stock.

The buy point can be looked at as the ground floor of a building where an elevator is about to rise to new highs. You do not only buy the right stock at the right price but also at the right time.

Cup with Handle Pattern

One of the most powerful patterns that allow consistency with stock purchase is the cup with handle pattern. This is the point where you buy a stock at its lowest price and is likely to rise very fast. Human nature is still the same where traders and other players in the markets exhibit either greed or fear.

What is Buy Point?

This is defined as the price level where stock is very likely to rise significantly. The buy point, also known as an entry point, is a point in the chart that offers the least resistance to a price increase.

Software for Technical Analysis

A key part of your life as a trader will involve the use of charts. In fact, there are those who believe that swing trader is only as productive as their charting software. You will spend a good amount of time reading charts and interpreting data on screens. Electronic trading platforms and market software are crucial resources of any serious trader. You can get most of the trading software from your preferred broker. There are other types of software programs available from software vendors. The trading software comes with a wide variety of functions including analysis functions, stock screening, research, and even trade.

In fact, trading software comes with in-built integrated additions like technical indicators, alert features, news, trade automation, fundamental analysis numbers, and much more.

Technical Analysis Charting Basics

Technical analysis is a method that answers the question of when to take or liquidate positions in markets or financial securities.

It does so by analyzing historical prices and trading volumes via price chart patterns and technical measures or indicators.

Technical analysis is grounded on key assumptions:

•   All possible information that can be gathered about a financial security or market, including financial and economic information, are already reflected on market prices, hence the focus on price;

•   Trading volume is a strong indicator of market interest or disinterest in financial securities;

•   Prices aren't as random as many think they are because it tends to follow general trends; and

•   Because prices follow patterns that tend to repeat themselves over time, traders can learn to anticipate price movements of financial securities with fairly high accuracy.

Double Bottoms and Double Tops

The difference between the 2 is that the double bottom refers to a stock or market that is in a downtrend and potentially signaling a reversal to the upside. A double top is an upward trending stock that is signaling the potential to turn and start a downtrend in price.

The double bottom pattern resembles the shape of a "W" when looked at in a chart. A stock in a downtrend reaches an initial bottom, bounces higher for a short period of time, and then retests the low it made on the initial bottom. There is some market psychology involved with this "W" pattern. Once the initial bottom is put in and the stock moves higher, the buyers of the stock at much higher prices may see the bounce as an opportunity to cut their losses and get out at this higher price (fearing the stock is going to continue lower). Others who bought in on the first bottom may be short-term holders who are happy to take their small gain on the bounce. As the stock price drops back after the initial bounce higher, the value investors may be looking to get a second chance at buying the stock at this lower price. These buyers wait and then buy in at the initial support level created by the first bottom. The stock then starts to move higher again and forms the familiar "W" pattern. Traders who have been short the stock may add to the buying pressure once they see a strong level of support has been established. This pattern also works in reverse. The double top forms an "M" pattern instead of a "W" in the chart. The initial push higher and subsequent pullback is seen by some investors as an opportunity to take an entry or add to their existing position. Unfortunately for these new longs, the first top acts as a level of resistance and the second attempt to move higher fails. Some traders who are long the stock will see this failure to break higher and start to sell. Other traders who short stocks might also start selling because they see that an area of resistance has developed. The added short selling will create additional downward pressure on the stock price. The stock then continues lower on a reversal in price action.

Establishing the stop price on your potential trade is the key to managing your account and the risk that you take in a trade. Once a double bottom pattern is traced out, the low on the "W" pattern becomes the stop-loss price. Prior levels of resistance can be established as exit points, thus making it possible to calculate a risk to reward ratio.

If you can catch an entry near the second bottom on a long trade, then the difference between your entry price and that bottom price on the "W" should be relatively low. That low price difference creates a situation where you do not require a lot of upside in the price to get that 2 times reward you need in order to make this a good trade. Getting a good entry on a stock can make a big difference in your risk to reward ratio. The opposite applies to taking a short trade on a double top. Try to get an entry as near as possible to the second top which should give you the most desirable risk to reward ratio. Your stop will be around the high price of the topping pattern. If the price does start to continue higher, you should cover your short promptly to limit your losses.

How to trade Flag Pattern?

The bull flag starts with a strong price spike higher that often catches traders who are short the stock off-guard. The many market scanners do their work and identify the long opportunity, so momentum traders then get in long to help feed the buying frenzy and push the price higher. The breakout happens when the upper resistance line is broken as the price surges higher again.

As the stock's price breaks through the high of the formation, it triggers yet another breakout and uptrend move. The sharper the spike higher on the flagpole, the more powerful the bull flag move can be.

Bull flag

The opposite of the bull flag is referred to as the bear flag. It has the same chart pattern as the bull flag except it is inverted and results in the continuation of downward price action in a stock. The upside down flagpole starts with an almost vertical price drop due to the sellers being firmly in control of the price action. Downward moves in price can be much more aggressive than upward price action. However, nothing drops forever and at some point the traders who shorted the stock look to cover their positions and the value investors see a potential opportunity.

Bear flag

Similar to the bull flag, if the support and resistance lines are closer to horizontal, then the 2 entry points will be closer as well.

Flag patterns require a little patience while you wait for the flag to form after the initial run up or drop. Once you have recognized the beginning of the pattern, you should start to plot the upper and lower trend-lines as they form. These trend-lines will be one of your potential entry points and/or stop out levels.

You will usually have 2 possible entry spots on any flag formation in order to play the continuation of the trend.

The first entry will get you into the position a little earlier, which will allow you to profit more on the next surge in price action (up or down). The downside of getting in earlier is that there is always the potential for the stock to have a failed breakout and not move in the direction you expect. Waiting a little longer for the break in the top of the flag results in a little higher probability of a successful trade.

These flag patterns also give you 2 stop-loss price level options to use in case the stock does not move in the direction expected. If the stock fails to follow through and continue the trend, then the trendlines can provide a price level for a stop. On a downtrend, you would use the upper resistance line in the flag and in an uptrend you would use the lower support line.

The second stop-loss option is to use the low of the lowest candle in the bull flag and the high of the highest candle in a bear flag.

If you are a more conservative trader, you would use the closer stop price to keep losses to a minimum. However, this may result in getting stopped out of a trade that is becoming more volatile as the trend starts to continue. This means that, while you may take a smaller loss with this stop out price level, using this level may result in missing the move you were intending to play by getting stopped out due to some volatility in price. This volatility component is why some traders will give the trade a little more room to avoid having their stop triggered due to some volatility as opposed to a real direction change. Therefore, they will place their stop at the lower support trendline on uptrends and at the higher resistance trendline on downtrends.

A more sophisticated or experienced trader might use multiple entries and exits to offset some of the risks of entering the trade too early. A smaller percentage of the total trade in shares can be used as a starter position and then added to at the second point above or below the flagpole.

After the reversal, there are several bear flags formed on the overall trend down as bargain hunters think the bottom is forming and they go long. Traders who went short at the double top start taking profits, giving a temporary lift in the stock's price before the selling continues.

Before you enter a flag pattern, as an effective swing trader you should also be planning your targeted exit price or prices. You should be expecting at least 2 times the reward for the given risk that you're taking in the event that you get stopped out. You should look at prior longer-term levels of resistance as possible exit points if you go long and areas of support to exit if you go short.

If you chose to enter at the break of the trend line, then your initial target can be set at the high or low of the flagpole. However, if the flag was close to horizontal, then that may not give you enough reward for the risk you are taking. You will have to look for other good exit points to get that 2 times reward you need to justify your trade.

Other factors you may want to consider are the strength of the trend, overall market trends and the possible strength of the fundamentals driving the move.

You may also consider scaling out of the position, which means taking some initial profits at the top of the flagpole by selling some of your position and then letting the remainder ride to your next expected level of resistance or support.

In this case, you must never let a winner turn into a loser. Lock in your profits and set your stop on the remainder at or near the entry price.

Bear and Bull Pendants

The bear and bull pendants are similar to the bear and bull flags described above. They start with a strong price move either up or down and then pause for a period of consolidation. The difference between the pendant and the flag is in the shape that the price action creates during this period of consolidation.

With a pendant, the range of price action narrows over the passage of time. When support and resistance lines are drawn off of the highs and lows, they come together in a point. The buyers and the sellers have been fighting it out and when the price action narrows to this point, often a winner finally emerges.

Usually the trend will continue after this narrowing period of consolidation, however, you should wait for a signal before taking an entry.

Do not assume that the trend will continue and take an early entry. While you wait for the pattern to play out, take time to look at the daily charts and identify areas of support and resistance that have occurred in the past.

Find potential profit target prices so you are prepared to do your risk to reward calculation in case you eventually consider an entry.

The narrowing price action is often compared to a coiled spring getting ready to pop one way or another.

You can find this narrowing price action on stocks that have been consolidating for days or weeks. These are also good stocks to watch because eventually either the buyers or sellers emerge in control and the ensuing price action can be strong.

ABCD Patterns

The ABCD pattern is another one of the basic and relatively easy patterns to recognize and trade. It is essentially a price move higher or lower, followed by a flag and then a continuation of a trend.

As with much technical analysis-based trading, it often works because so many traders and computers are watching for the pattern and subsequently trading this setup.

This pattern is based on the principle that stock prices move in waves. These waves are due to the fact that price control is continually moving between the buyers and the sellers. If you examine a daily price chart of any stock, you will see waves of fluctuation up and down.

Then, if you compare that daily chart to a weekly chart of the same stock, you will also see waves, but they will likely have larger price ranges because you're looking at a longer period of time. Within each one of those weekly bars there are 5 1-day bars, creating smaller waves inside bigger waves.

Knowing that stocks are moving in waves allows you to play on those waves much like a surfer. As a swing trader, you are waiting to catch and ride a wave, but like surfing, timing is very important. You will never see a surfer starting to paddle like crazy at the top of a wave to catch a ride.

They wait to begin their ride as the wave is just starting to approach. Similarly, a trader needs to anticipate the next wave and get on board at the beginning of the next move in price action.

Bullish ABCD patterns start with a strong upward move. The buyers are aggressively buying a stock from point A and consistently making new highs of the day (point B). You should not enter the trade here because at point B the price action is very extended. More importantly, your stop-loss will be way below your entry, giving you an extremely poor risk to reward ratio.

At point B, the traders who bought the stock earlier start selling it for profit and the price comes down. You should still not enter the trade because you do not know where the bottom of this pullback will be. However, if you see that the price does not come down from a certain level, such as point C, it means that the stock has found a potential support.

Bearish ABCD patterns are the reverse of the bullish pattern, with the stock price heading lower initially, and then there will be a bounce, which will be followed by a continuation lower.

The price action on this stock creates a very tradable pattern for a short trade. AMD pulls back from a high at point A to level B. It then forms a nice bear flag and also creates a double top when it fails to break through the previous high.

The stop-out price level on the short would be a break higher at about the $12.50 level. A failure of the stock to move higher would have allowed you to hold the position as it moved lower, possibly scaling out instead of selling the position for a profit all at once. By scaling out, you can lock in some profits and keep moving the stop out price lower as the price moves lower to maximize the gain on the trade.

How to Trade ABCD Patterns

The real key to trading this pattern is to watch for the pullbacks that inevitably occur when a stock makes a push higher or lower.

These patterns will often end with a double top or double bottom pattern. A topping pattern will usually have one or more gravestone type doji and the price action will struggle to make a new high and then ultimately fail and move lower. A bottoming pattern will be the reverse – one or more doji will make a dragonfly pattern signaling that the sellers are exhausted and the buyers are starting to take control. These signals do not necessarily have to appear but they help to confirm a setup for an entry on a trade.

Head and Shoulders Patterns

The head and shoulders chart pattern can be a top reversal signal and the so-called "inverted" head and shoulders pattern can be a bottom reversal pattern. This pattern is generally thought to be one of the most reliable swing trading patterns and therefore should be on your radar for stocks tracing out this type of price action.

The general pattern for the topping head and shoulders starts with a general uptrend in price action, which hits a peak and then slightly falls back or chops sideways for a period of time.

The stock then pushes higher through the previous peak and makes a new high before failing once again. Selling price action takes the stock back to the previous low after the first peak and the price action stays flat or bounces a little.

This price action in a chart traces the outline of a head and 2 shoulders; thus the name. A horizontal trend-line can be drawn across the 2 lows on the pullbacks and is referred to as the neckline. Once the price of the stock drops below this neckline, an established downtrend is in place and shorting the stock is now a tradable option.

Swing-Trading Rules

Simple Rules of Swing Trading

Rules are always there to help you be disciplined in what you are doing. Have you ever come across the swing trading rules before starting on trading? This chapter is all about covering the different rules of swing trading. The rules will guide you on the best ways on how to yield huge profits and incur minimum losses from swing trading. Below are some of the rules that will help you in your swing trading.

Simple Rules of Swing Trading

✔   **Select Volatile Markets.**

There are different markets in swing trading. To be successful in swing trading and be able to earn huge profits, you ought to choose a market with wider price fluctuations as compared to the narrower ones.

✔   **Consider Consistency.**

Consistency is the key to swing trading. You need to have a swing trading routine and always stick to it. Be consistent in what you are doing to prevent confusion and messing everything up. You ought to do much practice on the swing trading market to be familiar with all tips and tricks to be implemented. Practice this with the mock accounts you are provided with by the different brokers.

Mock accounts perfect your skills by providing virtual money to trade with. Be consistent with this practice before entering the real swing trading. Real trading in the swing market is all full of risks so you need to be fully prepared before making up your mind to start off.

✔ **Be Aware of Market Situations.**

A swing trading market has different situations. The market can either be bullish or bearish. You need to be aware of the market you are dealing with. Bearish markets are normally weak as compared to bullish markets. Be aware of the situation you are in the market so that you are able to make proper estimates of your profits and losses.

✔ **Do Not Take Chances.**

Do not be in the rush of making good money within a short period. Good things take time. Do not associate yourself in swing trading with gambling. You will lose a lot. Have patience with the money you are receiving, and with time, the money will of course increase. Do not utilize the chances since they will make you lose all the money that you worked hard for.

✔ **Accumulate Profits.**

Making a profit is always the main objective of any kind of business. You need to have a way of handling your profits made in swing trading. Profits need to be accumulated using different market strategies to prevent losses. The different market strategies may include implementing stop-loss orders on the stock when it reaches its resistance levels.

✔ **Be Aware of the Support and Level of Resistance.**

Support and the level of resistance are very crucial in swing trading. The stock in the swing trading market needs to be monitored. You need to be aware of its support and the level of resistance. The level of support and resistance on the stock are the prices on the trading chart at which a trader is able to tell if you have more buyers than sellers. The two factors aid to control the number of losses in the market.

✔ **Set Your Entry and Exit Points.**

Having an entry and exit plans in swing trading are very crucial. Sometimes the market behavior may not be as favorable as you accepted. Things and activities may go in vain. You need to have a plan to escape from this when it happens. Exit and entry point now come in handy. You are able to know how to work things out when the market is in its worst-case scenario. Always ensure to enter into the swing trading market with entry or exit plans to shun from making huge losses.

✔ **Take Advantage of the Stop-Loss Strategy.**

This is the kind of swing trading strategy that makes you be able to exit your position in the market. Stop-loss order when buying the stock is normally implemented at a position which allows a little change in the price fluctuations but becomes unfavorable when the market gets out of control.

Most swing traders purchasing stock use stop-loss when the price of the stock drops on the market.

Contrarily, when selling stock in the swing trading market, a stop-loss order can be implemented when there is a rise in the price of the stock since this is the resistance level of the underlying stock.

✔ **Minimize Losses.**

Losses are normally part of the game, but you need to do something when they become out of control. Losses affect your profits and your trading capital. You need to have some various working strategies on how to get rid of the losses in swing trading. Always implement the strategies when trading to succeed. If things are not working out well as expected, you need to quit what you are doing and work on something else.

Losses can make you lose a lot of money if you are not cautious while trading. The objectives of swing trading are all about raising profits and making investments and not making losses.

✔ **Have Control of Your Emotions.**

Do you know that emotions have made many traders fail in their trading? Emotions should not be part of any trader in the swing trading. Swing trading markets have both best-case and worst-case scenarios. You need to control your emotions when both scenarios happen in the market. You do not need to get over-excited when the market goes according to your favor. You need to be always alert not to drop tremendously.

Also, during your worst-case scenarios, do not get carried away with your emotions. Be strong and stop with the crying.

When things do not work out as you expected, find alternative actions immediately to be implemented in the market to avoid huge losses and risks in the swing trading market.

Do not feel bad when the mistakes happen in your trading, they are normally part of being successful in swing trading. Learn from the previous mistakes made to avoid repeating the mistakes next time you are trading. Mistakes normally make you grow and you learn a lot.

✔ **Have a Trading Plan.**

Who starts off something without a plan? You need to have a plan for everything. Swing trading requires a plan too. A trading plan guides you in all your activities. You are able to know the actions to be implemented in different market situations. A trading plan provides you with the desired market strategies and also assist in raising a reasonable amount of capital. A trading plan provides a routine for you and helps you become disciplined when you are trading.

A trading plan creates a schedule for your trading, in terms of the time and the type of trading you are dealing with. Also, a plan also enables you to come up with the goals and objectives of your trading. Objectives help you put much effort so as to achieve the goals. Do not enter into the swing trading market without a plan, it is a crucial factor that needs to be integrated with your trading.

✔ **Enjoy Swing Trading.**

Why does something you do not enjoy? Swing trading requires much passion when practicing it.

You need to be love spending much of your time on your computer since most of the swing trading markets are online platforms. You need to be excited when trading. This will motivate you to learn more about it and you will get much informed. Knowledge is powerful since it leads to success.

Do your trading with all the passion and enjoy it. You can also join forums with swing traders' experts to learn and see what others are doing. Swing trading is not an easy thing, you need to have much love and passion for it to succeed. A bored swing trader gets tired with time and decides to give up with trading. Be the happy trader and success will definitely come your way.

✔ **Come up with Good Swing Trading Decisions.**

The kind of decisions you make in trading defines you a lot. Do you expect success when you come up with poor decisions? A swing trader needs to make strong and good decisions while trading. You need to prepare yourself so well mentally on the best thing to do when the different market situations occur.

Do not be the kind of trader who makes poor and rushing decisions when things fall apart. Be a good decision-maker for better success in the future. Also, do not rely so much on what people are saying online. You need to come up with your own decisions for your own trading. Others may mislead you and this might make you fail terribly. Be strong and do the right thing.

The Swing Trader Mindset

Beginners are prone to making mistakes in any endeavor. The problem with the stock market is making mistakes can be extremely costly when you are a trader, even leading to bankruptcy. Nevertheless, by learning from the mistakes of others, you can avoid falling prey to the biggest problems that might come your way as a result of your inexperience.

Failing to exit a losing trade

It can't be said enough; all too often people let emotions take over their judgment in the stock market. When you set up a big swing trade, you might get overconfident and excessively excited about it if you are new to the business. Moreover, if the stock starts moving the wrong way, you might hold onto the trade when you should simply exit and take your losses. Sometimes people can't believe it when a "sure thing" turns out to be a loss, and they hold on too long hoping things are going to turn around. Waiting too long can be costly – sometimes catastrophically so. We hate to beat a dead horse – but protect every trade you make with stop-loss orders rather than letting emotion take over.

Exiting Too Soon

The right time to exit a trade can be a difficult thing to figure out. That's why it's best to plan ahead of time and set an exit point where you are going to be comfortable with profits.

If you go into a swing trade without a definite plan, it's going to be too

easy to fall prey to a situation where you might get out too soon, afraid that you aren't going to be able to make any profit and fearing possible losses. You can also get fooled by temporary downturns. Remember that there are always counter trends on the way up. Don't be fooled by the counter trends into exiting too early. Emotion can get heavy immediately after placing a big trade. Also, remember that you should set a time frame for your trade to work out. Swing traders are not day traders, so don't get the impulse to exit a trade two hours after you've entered the position.

Believing shares won't lose value

Unbelievably, some people have the same attitude about stocks that people used to have about housing, which is that stocks won't decline. Sometimes they do, and they don't recover. Just because it's Google or Apple, it doesn't mean that losses aren't possible.

Too much margin

Swing traders can actually access a lot of margins. That means that you can borrow to buy shares from the broker. That can be a problem if you end up losing big, you might end up owing the broker a large amount of money. You need to be extremely careful with margin, and all things considered, it is better to grow slowly by making methodical trades with money you already have than it is to borrow lots of money in hope of quickly growing your account.

Waiting too long for price declines

There are ideal price points to buy shares. However, you shouldn't always wait to reach a level of support before buying. Sometimes a stock might be entering an upward trend, and it's going to establish a new level of support. If you wait too long hoping the price is going to drop down to the last level of support, you might miss out on the opportunity.

Believing past performance is a guarantee of future performance

This is one of the biggest fallacies of the stock market. You cannot take the past performance of a company's stock as an ironclad guarantee that the stock is going to perform the same way going forward. Past performance indicates little compared to the company's current fundamentals, trading volume, volatility, and the trends and indicators for the stock in the here and now. Just because Amazon grew a lot in the past five years, it doesn't mean it will continue to do so.

Investing more than you can afford to lose

It's easy to get excited about the amount of money you can make swing trading, and it's also easy to get excited over all the charts, all the action, and the thrills of making winning trades. This can lead some people into pulling out too much money from savings and retirement accounts to enter into larger trades. That is a big mistake.

You should always keep in mind that you need to set up trades where you can afford to lose it all, so your personal savings, college savings accounts, and retirement accounts won't be impacted, and you won't have trouble paying for your basic living expenses. Set aside the excitement and prepare for a long journey where you grow your business slowly, so you don't end up in the poor house.

Get started with small and achievable profit goals, and when your trades go bad as some inevitably will, your losses will be minimal.

Now we'll look at the swing trader mindset. This will be a mix of characteristics and attitudes you should have before even becoming a swing trader, and also a set of behaviors and mindsets you should adopt once you become a swing trader.

You must be Risk Tolerant

Most investors have a low tolerance for risk. That is why they put money in savings accounts and mutual funds. Becoming a swing trader can be said to put you in an elite community. That isn't to say that swing traders are better people. What we mean by this is that swing trader are a small group relative to the overall population. The vast majority of people are not willing to risk their capital in order to realize large, short-term gains. While a swing trader is more cautious (and some would say more rational) than a day trader, compared to the average outlook that most people have if you are interested in swing trading that indicates a much higher tolerance of risk.

You are not ruled by emotion

A successful swing trader is not going to be someone who is ruled by emotion. You are going to enter into and exit your trades based on a cold, hard examination of the facts.

Someone who is caught up in emotion when stocks start moving up fast or sliding down is not someone who is suitable to be a swing trader.

Emotional decisions can lead to many bad trades and can even be catastrophic. The average person can panic when a certain trend appears in the stock market. There is no room for panic if you decide to become a trader, keeping a cool head at all times is essential.

You do your homework

A swing trader is not going to trade based on their gut. That is something amateurs do. Of course, we always hear the winning stories, but most of the time people trading on their gut are going to lose out.

As a successful swing trader, you should be trading based on a thorough background check of the situation. You should be doing your homework by picking 2-3 of your favorite technical analysis tools, studying candlesticks and trends, and also studying the fundamentals of the company and keeping up with financial news.

 Only after you've thoroughly evaluated a stock should you consider entering into a trade. People who don't do their homework might win some of the time, but at the end of a year when you compile all the wins and losses, people that don't do their homework are going to finish last unless they got very lucky.

The world isn't governed by luck unless you're at a gambling casino. Despite the unfair reputation, trading might have among the ignorant public, swing trading is not gambling, and so isn't governed by luck.

You are disciplined

A swing trader is disciplined. This really follows on the heels of the previous point, but a swing trader is someone that studies everything carefully and takes the time to study all of the technical analysis indicators and trends they are going to use in their analysis. Then you will have the discipline to develop a trading plan, and you're going to have the discipline to stick to the trading plan. When becoming a swing trader, whether you're going to do it full-time or only on a part-time basis keeping your day job, you need to look at swing trading as a business. You wouldn't run a business based on temporary emotional outbursts. If you did, you could easily end up broke. For example, suppose you find some kind of craft made in China and open a shop to sell them. The third day your shop is open; someone comes in and praises them and buys three. You get super excited. Do you then take your entire life savings and buy 1,000 more? We hope not.

Swing trading needs to be approached in the same way. View it as a business and make a business plan that you are going to follow. You are not going to get rattled by missing out on potential gains in the share price.

For one thing, until any gains happen, they are nothing but imaginary. It is better to sell when you can do so and take a profit. Second, you are not in this to make a large profit off one trade. Of course, if you have a great trade, all the more power to you. However, generally speaking, swing trading is about earning money steadily from trades over the long term and slowly growing your business. It is not a get rich quick scheme, so don't think of it that way. If you can make a $1,000 profit from a trade, you are doing quite well, and you can reinvest the money to continue to grow your business with time. Any time you are making profits from a trade, it is going to be a time to be happy, even if it is only $100.

Amateurs are the ones who are going to fret because they "missed out." More often than not, share prices are going to drop off from some peak if you hold on too long, and you will miss out on what you could have had if only you had the discipline to sell at the right time. That is more dangerous than missing out on some "big thing" that could have netted you huge returns.

You prepare for all outcomes

As part of running your swing trading as a business, a good swing trader prepares for all outcomes. That is why we included the one order cancels another approach in this book. Everyone expects profits, but they don't always materialize. Therefore, you need to be as prepared for losses - in fact, more so – as well as being prepared to cash in profits.

Preparing for all outcomes means first determining the risk level you are willing to accept for your account. You have to set a risk level you are comfortable with, the 1-2% level is recommended by market experts, but that doesn't mean you have to follow it exactly. However, no matter what you do need to set a level of risk so that if you did lose the capital, you are not going to be hurt financially. Of course, any loss of capital hurts, but you shouldn't be having to go into debt or begging on the street corner to make your house payment because you made a bad trade. You also need to make sure that not only are your losses not catastrophic, but if you do take a loss, you still have enough money to enter into another trade.

Also, be aware of creeping losses. If you keep losing $500 per trade without making any gains, you need to take a look at your trading

 practices and dial back your level of risk. A $500 loss one time is one thing, a $500 loss every week can add up fast.

You can adjust your strategy

Emotion can take over in many ways when trading. Money has that effect on people. One way that emotion can overtake you is if you develop your own system for swing trading, and you start making multiple winning trades.

Then something in the market might change, and maybe you start losing lots of money. In that case, are you going to be beholden to your old system, or adjust to the changing conditions?

A successful trader is going to be one who makes the adjustments. Don't take it personally, when things stop working. Always fall back on doing the analysis, remember that hard facts rule the day at all times, not your love of Apple, Netflix, or even your own trading methods.

You might also take a look at what indicators you are using. Maybe it's time to try different indicators. On the other hand, maybe you are even relying on indicators too much, or putting too much stock in trends.

Successful traders don't stop learning

This book should be taken as your first step. A successful trader is one who is open to continuous education. There are always things to learn from others that can help make you a better trader. You should be putting in an effort to educate yourself to grow your knowledge about finance, the stock market, and business.

That includes watching YouTube videos, taking courses, and reading as many books about the subject as you can. You should also watch plenty of financial news so you can learn about current conditions and how people think they are going to change. They aren't always going to be right, but the more knowledge you have, the better positioned you are going to be when it comes to being a successful trader.

Don't give in to euphoria or despair

We are all going to have big winning trades and massive losses at one point or another if we trade for any length of time. Whether you experience a big loss or not is not the question, it's how you react to it. Persistence and objective analysis about what went wrong with the trade are the proper ways to respond. Falling into emotional despair is unproductive and doesn't help the situation. First off, if you give in to emotional despair, you are not going to learn from your mistakes. You are also letting your emotions take over and take control of your actions. Of course, if you have followed the principles outlined in this book, you won't have any catastrophic losses – but if you do then review the principles behind managing risk, dust yourself off and try again.

Euphoria over a big winning trade can be as damaging. Book your winning trades and be happy about them, but don't let yourself be overcome by mania.

Also, don't waste money.

Sure, you can take a little out to celebrate, but again, you should treat this as a business and reinvest most of your profits. Long-term growth of your business should be the number one goal. If you are living off your trades, only take out what you need to take out. Don't blow a winning trade on a new car and a trip to Europe. It's also important because it might lead you into entering into a lot of bad trades in the aftermath. Sometimes people can get overconfident and then blow themselves out of the water because they let their euphoria take over and they overtraded.

Swing Trading Strategies

You've probably been reading this book and wondering at what point we will start to talk about swing trading strategies.

After all, you are probably most interested in the actual strategies that you can apply to make money swing trading. You can see though, that there is a lot to learn before you can start to understand the strategies that people use to swing trade. The market has many factors at play, and you need to understand the tools used to assess companies and their technical movements. You won't be able to use the same strategy in every situation, so knowing how to read the market is the first step before learning strategy.

The indicators that you are looking for will depend on the type of strategy you are using, so pay close attention to the fundamental characteristics of companies and you'll start to recognize similarities amongst different opportunities.

The first step is to make a habit of mining for opportunities. There are a lot of fascinating economic and business journals available on the internet that you can peruse for information about current events and finance news.

You never know how you will identify your next opportunity. An article about energy companies in Texas may inspire you to research energy contracts in the American Southwest, and which companies to watch for.

An article in a tech news magazine might send you on a hunt for publicly traded companies developing a certain type of computer hardware. If it intrigues you, then let yourself be drawn in for further research. The important thing is to spend a little time each day reading and identifying possible opportunities. Once you've noticed an opportunity, dig a little deeper and review the company's involved and check out their fundamentals. How have these companies been performing? Is it worth taking a position?

You can do this research by looking at the market sector by sector. Find indexes that represent different sectors you are interested in and check up with them every day. It's good to have a relatively broad field of interests from which you can identify options. One sector might be ripe with opportunities while another sector lags on the same day. Being able to switch gears and focus on the place where opportunities are happening will make you a more effective and well-rounded trader.

The type of strategy you use will also affect what characteristics you'll be looking for. If you are willing to take on a little more risk and you want to try swing trading, then you will be looking for stocks that show signs of a moving downwards. With the uptick rule, you will have to find stocks that are moving up now, but you have reason to believe that they will continue to drop in the future.

If you want to buy a stock and hang on to it and make a profit, then you'll be looking for stocks or sectors that are healthy and have continued and consistent growth.

The earlier you enter a position, the better.

Look out for signs of reversals as both a short seller and a bull trader. The sooner you enter a position after a true reversal, the more you can earn.

Remember the tenet of Dow Theory that states that the average of all the stocks in the index should confirm each other. You may just take a position on one or two stocks, but its good to have a picture of the entire sector. This will tell you whether you will be swimming upstream or downstream. It's OK to swim upstream as long as you feel like you have a compelling reason.

When you have identified a stock that balances risk and reward ratio, decide what price you'd like to buy-in. This will require some research into the fundamentals of a company so you can evaluate whether you are overpaying or underpaying.

One strategy that you can employ as a swing trader is known as gap trading. A gap is when there is a significant difference between the closing price of a stock today, and the opening price of that stock tomorrow. As a swing trader, you can try and take advantage of these gaps by anticipating that gap and choosing a favorable position. There are instances when the gap could go against you; like with a secondary offering or a bad financial report. But there are just as many instances when you can try to predict a gap.

Swing traders have an advantage over day traders because they can use this gap.

Day traders are also less susceptible to the risk that the gap creates.

Depending on your outlook and your strategy, you may see the gap as either a good thing or a bad thing. Unfortunately, with gap trading, you don't have much control if the stock price moves against your position. You just must wait for the market to open the next day in order to react.

Gaps could open in several ways. A company could release a statement of earnings, and as a result, the price of the stock could drop or go up significantly in a short amount of time. Unfortunately, it's hard to anticipate a company's earnings report in order to make an educated guess on a good position. Most investors consider it to be too risky to play the gap on an earnings report because it's too easy for there to be a surprise when the company releases its statement.

Another way to take advantage of a gap is by researching companies that are developing new technologies. This type of stock can be very volatile, with attitudes changing swiftly about the predicted success or failure of the product. The volatility could be an opportunity for the swing trader if they timed it right. Just be aware of the way the market can respond to an announcement about new technology. The stock price may shoot up to unprecedented levels as a result but often, things will settle down shortly after. Knowing how to time a position during a product announcement will be a major factor in whether you stand to make any money.

Remember; not all products succeed either. Sometimes a new product can hurt the company, in the long run, more than it helps them in the short run. Imagine an automotive company that announces the release of a new model. For a while, the model could increase anticipated earnings and investors might flock to the company. But the first model of the car might have more issues than expected, and the safety rating may be lower than normal. Remember that Dow Theory says that every action results in a reaction on the market. A product that performs poorly can do just as much harm as a product that performs well. Keep track of the progress of the companies in your portfolio, and make sure you time your positions well.

Another way a swing trader can ride a trend is to seek industries that are experiencing booms. Look for industries that are 'trendy'. Right now, the marijuana industry is experiencing a major boom and investors who recognized the possibilities of this trend early are enjoying a growing portfolio. With the legalization of Marijuana in Canada and many states in the US, there are new companies popping up all over as demand for the product is growing. Eventually, there could be a bubble once the expansion adjusts. But trends like these present opportunities for swing traders. Whether or not you decide to invest in the marijuana industry, its an example of a rideable trend. Who knows how it could play out?

These opportunities that exist in trends don't come around too often, and a swing trader must be patient in order to identify them.

Usually, though, all one needs to do to find out about these trends is read the newspaper. Trends come and go and the window for making a real profit is limited. But if you're patient then there will always be another trend around the corner. The trick is to keep your ears to the wind so that you know when an opportunity has arrived.

Just like any swing trading strategy, a lot of it comes down to timing. A good example of a famous trend is the dotcom bubble in the 90s and early 2000s. A lot of people made big off the rise in internet technologies and computer companies. Eventually, though, the trend took a major dip and there were just as many losers from the dot-com trend as there were winners. Just remember that the stock market works in cycles and patterns, and these patterns often repeat themselves. Monitor your positions and stay up to date on news cycles.

When it comes to deciding on a position, timing is important. This means not only timing your exit but also timing your entry. It's better to be patient and wait for a good opportunity to buy when the stock price is low than to try and rush in out of impatience.

Before you open a position decide how much you are willing to pay. This is important because when you have a target price you can calculate exactly what you are risking before you even take on a position.

Again, it's better to figure this out before you even take the position.

Once you've determined an entry point then you must be patient.

Wait for the price of the stock to match your ideal price. If it doesn't, then move on. Never forget that being a good trader requires discipline, which includes knowing when you should take an opportunity and when you should look at other options.

There are ways to track the price or set entry points without the need to constantly monitor the market. For example, a lot of brokerages offer alert services where you can receive notifications when the price of a stock has reached a predetermined target. You decide on an entry point and go about your day, then you receive a notification from your broker. You can even give them a limit order, which tells your broker to buy the stock for you once it hits that target. These notifications are also available for sale targets, so your broker can let you know when the stock has reached that target. They can even sell it automatically for you.

You've read about setting an exit point by now, and how sometimes you'd like to leave some flexibility in case the stock price continues to move in your favor. One way to do this is by not exiting your position all at once. Let's say you a buy a stock and the price of that stock has risen beyond your exit point and it is still moving. You want to preserve some of your earnings, but you are also curious about how high the stock might go. You take to exit your position with only a portion of your money while leaving the rest in. You slowly withdraw your position in increments, but you maintain some percentage of your position until you are completely ready to withdraw. This technique is called scaling out.

Intermediate and Advanced Trading Strategies

Throughout this guidebook, we have spent some time taking a look at some of the different things that you can do when it comes to trading with swing trading.

Now, it is time to take it a bit deeper and look at some of the more intermediate and advanced trading strategies that you can use. As you progress with your swing trading, get a better idea of how it works, and are ready to take it a bit further to see what results you can get, these strategies are going to be the best options for you. Some of the different advanced trading strategies that you can use with swing trading include the following.

Moving Average Trend Trading

The first strategy that we are going to take a look at here is the moving average trend strategy. This moving average is important because it is going to be the way that you can pick out when you want to enter and when you want to exit a trade for a specific stock. There are many stocks that are going to start out the morning doing well in the morning trend, and they will have a strong upside or downside trend. You would then watch their charts and see where the moving averages go in the charts. This is beneficial to the traders because you will then be able to follow the moving average to figure out which trend is occurring and you can ride out that kind of trend.

While this strategy does sound like it takes a bit of time to figure out and it may seem complicated to work with, it is pretty easy to learn how to use properly.

Some of the steps that are needed to make this one work for your needs include:

•	When you take a look at the graphs that you want to use and you are checking out the stock you want to use, make sure that you look to see whether or not a trend is forming near the spot that is the moving average. When you do see this, you will want to get into the market and use this strategy. You can then spend a bit of time looking at the trading data that shows up for that stock from the day before. This is important to see how the moving average changes and how the stock is going to respond to that average.

•	After looking over the charts and getting a chance to see which moving average is the best one for the trade you are doing, it is time to make a purchase of the stock. Some traders do choose to wait a little bit longer in order to confirm the moving average before they enter. But, either way, try to purchase as close to the lines for the moving average as you can.

•	Once you are ready, you need to pick out the stop points that you want to use. You may want to consider setting the stop just a bit below the moving average line to help protect your investment, but it still allows for a little bit of volatility of movement.

If you are doing this strategy with a candlestick chart, then you need to make sure that you have a start that is close to the moving average and choose to work with a long position.

• After you have these in place and have been able to enter the market, you can just ride on that trend until you see the moving average break and then take your profits.

For this kind of strategy, it is important to remember that you never want to work with a trailing stop on this strategy. This one is also a strategy where you need to pay full attention to the market or more than usual because there are times when the market can end up getting away from you.

While the scanner can be great for helping you get the right trades, you need to make sure that you use your own eyes rather than the scanner when you are ready to use this kind of strategy.

If you see that your chosen stock is moving really high from the moving average, this means that you are making a great profit. At this time, it may be best to take the half position rather than going all the way to your break. This is going to make sure that you make some profit, and sometimes, you will see the moving trend go down before the break. If you let this happen, it is possible to lose out on all of the profit. But, with the half position, you can at least make some profit.

Resistance Trading

The next option that we are going to take a look at when it comes to trading is the resistance trading strategy.

Support and resistance trading are also very popular when it comes to doing swing trading; you will probably find a lot of traders who choose to work with this method instead of one of the others. The support is going to be the price level when buying is really strong, so strong that it can interrupt or reverse the current downtrend that may show up in the charts.

When your current downtrend gets to a support level, it is going to bounce back at least a little. When you are looking at your graphs, this support line is going to be shown on a chart with a horizontal line that needs to connect together at least two bottoms together.

Then, we have to take a look at the resistance, which is going to be the opposite. This will end up being the price level where you see a strong selling position, one that is so strong that it can reverse the uptrend that is going on in the charts. When you see the uptrend hit this level, the trend is going to stop, and sometimes, it will go down. The resistance is going to be represented similar to the support, but it will connect together two or more tops.

In some cases, it is possible to get a minor resistance or a minor support. These are going to cause a little pause in the trend. But, when you work with the major support or resistance, it is going to be able to force the trend to reverse. Traders who are working with this kind of strategy will try to make a purchase as close to the support as possible, and then, they will sell as close to the resistance as possible. This helps them to get the most out of each trade.

In order to figure out these support and resistance levels, you need to take some time to look at the daily charts of your chosen stocks. Sometimes, this line is even hard to find, and you may have to wait a few days in order to find a clear line that you are comfortable using. This means that patience is needed with this kind of strategy as you may have to wait a bit to get started with this strategy at all.

There are some steps that you can use the charts that you have available to help draw your own support and resistant lines. Some of the steps you can take to make this process easier and to really use this **strategy include:**

•   Remember those indecision candles? You are going to see these in areas of support and resistance. These candles often show that buyers and sellers are fighting with each other to see who has the most control over the price.

•   Often, half dollars and whole dollars can be good support and resistance levels. This is especially true when you work on stocks under $10. If you can't find your support or your resistance lines, check here and see if your line would work there.

•   When you make your own lines, you need to have the most recent data available. This ensures that you are getting the best information for that stock.

•   The more that your line is able to touch the extreme price of the stock, the better option this line is for your support and resistance. If it is too far from this extreme point, then it is not going to have enough value to make it strong.

- Only look at any support or resistance lines that stay with the current price range. For example, if the stock's price is around $20 right now, you do not need to look at the region on the graph where the stock randomly jumped up to $40. This is not an area where the stock will probably go back to, so it doesn't make much sense to work from there.

- Many times, the support and resistance is not just one exact number. Often, it is more of an area. If you come up with a support or resistance that is about $19.69, then you know that the movement is somewhere near that number and not exactly that number. You can usually estimate that the area is going to be somewhere between five to ten cents above or under that line.

- The price that you want to work from will need to have a clear bounce off that level. If you can't find that this price bounces at that level, then this is not a good support or resistance level for you to work with. Your levels need to be really easy to notice and need to make sense for the charts you look at. If you have any questions about whether you picked the right one or not, it's not the right one.

When you go onto the charts and create these lines, you may find that drawing the perfect line can be a challenge. You need to make sure that you are picking out the right lines for the support and for the resistance so that you know how to base the trades. But, the best way to ensure that you are doing this the proper way is to take the time to practice. Over time, you will get better, and this will be a great strategy to go with.

Opening Range Breakout

The next strategy that we are going to take a look at when it comes to advanced strategies for swing trading is known as the opening range breakout. This strategy is a great one to work with because it provides you with a good signal for when to enter the market, but it does make it more difficult to know where you should target the profit. You have to go through and do some of the work on your own, and you can pick out the profit that you would like this trade to reach based on some of the other strategies that we have discussed. The opening range breakout is often one that a trader is going to use if they need a good signal for entry, but you will then need to come up with the right exit point for your trades as well.

To work with this kind of strategy, you need to pay a lot of attention to what shows up in the market. When you are taking a look at some of the stock charts at this time, you may see that the Stocks in Play are going to have some violent price action. Buyers and sellers are going to flood the market during the first five to ten minutes when the market opens. This can be a very crazy time to trade. New investors are often going to stay out of the market during this time because it is too volatile for them to see results.

But, there are some investors who are going to take a look at this market opening and decide that their position did go down during the night. There are some who will panic because they don't realize what is going on at this time, and they will try to sell their stocks and hopefully make something.

There are also a lot of new investors who will come to the market at this time, see that the stock is being offered at a discount from the panicked seller, and will purchase the stock at that great deal. Both of these movements are going to be important because they are going to help you determine the price of the stock, and it gives you a good idea of what is going to happen during that day.

As a swing trader, it is important to wait out that first little bit of the market. It is often best to wait at least the first fifteen minutes or so before entering the market. This ensures that you don't get stuck in the market and run into trouble along the way as well. You want to wait until after all the craziness has had some time to pass before you try to join the market and end up getting in on the wrong side of a position.

Like with many of the other setups that we have talked about in this guidebook, the opening range breakout strategy is going to work the best with either mid-cap or large stocks or ones that won't go through huge and unpredictable price swings while you hold onto them.

You also want to make sure that you don't go into this type of strategy with some low float stocks. Pick out a stock that has the ability to trade inside a range smaller than the ATR or the Average True Range.

When working with the opening range breakout strategy, there are a few steps that you will need to follow.

These steps include:

- After you have had some time to create your watchlist in the morning, you should wait until the stock market has had time to settle down, so wait about five minutes. During this time, watch the price action and the opening range. You can also check out how many shares are traded during that time and then figure out from that information if the stock is going down or up. This time is when a ton of orders go through the market and you want to look at these numbers to see how liquid a stock actually is.

- During this time, you can also look through to see what the ATR of that stock is. You want the opening range to be smaller compared to the ATR so make sure that the ATR number is nearby.

- Once those first five minutes of market opening are finished, you may see that the stock will stay in that opening range a bit longer depending on what traders and investors want to do. However, if you see at this time that the stock is breaking out of this range, it is time to enter the trade. Enter the trade going the same direction of the breakout. If you can, go long if you see the breakout is going up, but go short if the breakout is going down.

- Pick out a good target for your profit as well. You can find this by looking at the daily levels from the previous day and identify where the stock is before the market opens. You can also look at the previous days' close, along with the moving averages, to come up with a good target.

- If you can't find the right technical level for your chosen target or for the exit, you can choose to go long and then look for signs of weakness. On the other hand, if you want to take a short position and then the stock goes high, this shows you the stock is strong, and you want to cover the position as much as you can.

You will want to work with this method whether you want to work with a shorter or a longer time frame. But, the steps above are done with a shorter trade of just one day. You can go in and expand it out to fit the needs that you have when it comes to swing trading.

Trend

Okay, we've looked at stages and waves. Now let's turn our attention to trends.

To put it simply, a trend is the relatively consistent price movement in one predominant direction within a particular time frame. These price movements could be either sideways, up, or down so long as they are fairly consistent for a considerable amount of time. Trends may last for as long as several months; a huge profit-making period for traders who can see the bigger picture.

Countertrends

It is possible to have a countertrend within a predominant trend (the bigger picture). This is not just a pullback or a rally; it is period where a trend goes in the opposite direction of a major trend for as long as several weeks or months. However, its price movements eventually return to the major trend. This is good for you as a swing trader because you are not in the market for the long-haul. So you can make a profit from both the predominant trend (bigger picture) and from the countertrend.

Short-term Trends

Within the predominant trend, there is also the possibility of having short-term trends which are super cool for swing traders.

Short-term trends can sometimes last for as long as several days to weeks.

But guess what: short-term trends are usually not apparent when you are looking at the bigger picture – the predominant trend. You need to zoom in closer to see them. So, take a look at any stock chart that shows a predominant trend for several months, but this time, magnify the chart to show you daily trends. You can zoom in closer to see hourly or shorter time periods. There you will find swing trading honeypots that are of no interest to the buy-and-hold investor, but which are goldmines to the swing trader!

Trending Stocks

As a beginner, if you really want to make money from swing trading over and over again, you should trade trending stocks (stocks that are in an uptrend or downtrend). And here is how to know a trending stock. A stock in an uptrend has higher highs and higher lows. In other words, a stock in the second stage is in an upward trend. Also, a stock in a downtrend has lower highs and lower lows. That is to say; fourth stage stocks are in a downward trend.

Generally, stocks are either in a trending phase or they are in a trading ranges phase. It has been roughly estimated that stocks are in the trending phase for about 30 percent of the time. The rest of the time, they are in the trading ranges phase.

Now take a good look at another chart below to see if, as a beginner, you would prefer to trade during a trending ranges phase.

Ignorance is what makes people who are new to swing trading enter trades during the trading ranges phase.

It is very risky because there is hardly a chance of predicting any trend up or down. Trading ranges usually occur during the first and third stages of a stock movement. Remember, we said that you should stay in cash (hold 'em) during these stages. One of the fastest ways to throw away your capital is to trade stocks when they are in the trading ranges phase.

A Note about "Buying Cheap"

When stocks are falling excessively (in a critical downtrend), a swing trader may be tempted to go long excessively (buy larger amounts of stock) because falling price means cheap stocks. I would recommend that you should be very careful when attempting to buy into such stocks. If you must buy, you should utilize stop orders. Let me briefly explain why.

You see, in the stock market, as well as with every other aspect of life, "cheap stocks" usually have a tendency of eventually becoming cheaper. It may not happen all of the time, but it does happen. However, there is a possibility of cheaper stocks to rebound. But it may take a long time for cheaper stocks to bounce back up; time which a swing trader does not have. In other words, if a swing trader rushes into "buying cheap" he or she may end up amassing cheap stocks that no one will be interested in buying back. I believe that is not your aim for venturing into swing trading, yes?

Bottom Line

Practice looking at charts and pinpointing whether they are in the trending or trade ranges phase.

It is a huge mistake to go long or buy a stock that is heading in a downtrend simply because you notice a sudden upward price movement. If the stock is truly in a downtrend, then the sudden upward price movement is a rally that doesn't last. It usually quickly returns downward, and that is a great time to go short (sell). The opposite applies to an uptrend. Do not go short because you observe a pullback. It usually bounces back in a short while.

The sudden downward price movement is an excellent time to go long (buy stocks) before the bounce back happens.

Conclusion

Traditionally swing trading continues to be described as a speculative technique as the roles are usually purchased as well as held for the trader's fixed timeframe.

These time frames could vary between 2 days to a couple of months. The objective of the swing trader is usually to determine the trend either up or maybe place and down the trades of theirs is probably the most advantageous position. From there the trader is going to ride the pattern to what they decide when the exhaustion point in addition to sell for an income. In many cases swing traders are going to utilize a variety of technical indicators that will enable them to have a far more advantageous probability when making the trades of theirs. Shorter-term traders don't always usually swing trade as they choose to hold positions during the day and working out them before the close of the marketplace. Swing trading tactic utilizes time and it's this time which will be the deterrent factor for most day traders. In many cases there's way too much risk associated with the close of the marketplace and that a trader won't be happy to accept this risk.

The distinction of swing trading is an extensive subject in its numerous various influences from a wide range of various trading methods. Every one of these trading techniques are unique and also have the respective risk profiles of theirs.

Swing trading is usually a great way for a market place participant to further improve the technical analysis skills of theirs while offering them a chance to pay a lot more focus on the essential side of trading.

Several effective swing traders have been recognized to utilize a Bollinger band program as a tool to help them in entering as well as exiting positions. Naturally, for a swing trader to achieve success in the technique, they are going to need to get an impressive aptitude for identifying the present industry trend and putting the positions of theirs in accordance with that pattern. It does a swing trader note great to put a brief position with the program of holding for a prolonged time period of a market place which is certainly trending upwards. The general theme here's the aim of the traders must be increasing the probability of theirs of success while limiting or even eliminating risk completely. The swing trader's most detrimental enemy is the fact that associated with sideways or in the market that is active. Sideways price actions are going to stop a swing trader cold in his or maybe the tracks of her as there's absolutely no prevailing pattern to key out of.

When utilized properly swing trading is a superb approach used by lots of traders across various different market segments. It's not just applied to the Forex market though it's a vital instrument of equity and futures markets. Swing traders take the abilities they discover through technical analysis and may also parlay these skills into different options strategies.

The short term dynamics of swing trading sets it apart from which of the standard investor. Investors generally have a longer term time horizon and aren't usually impacted by short-term price fluctuations.

Of course, one must keep in mind that swing trading is just one strategy and must be utilized just when appropriately understood.

Like every trading strategies swing trading is able to be conservative and risky strategies can become day trading strategies rather quick. In case you plan to use a swing trading program, make sure that you completely grasp the risks and create a method that will have the opportunity to enable you to produce optimum portion returns on the positions of yours.

Swing trading is 1 of trading types which generally implemented in speculative activity in monetary markets like bonds, foreign exchange, commodity, stock as well as inventory index. Generally this trading design takes a swing trader to keep his or maybe her trading job over one trading day, often two to five trading days. Swing trading is common in the trading community as this particular trading types normally have an excellent reward and risk ratio, it indicates the probability to increase profit is bigger compared to the chance that could increase in each trade.

Generally, swing trading aims for a hundred pips earnings probability. Benefit potential could be acquired from every industry swing. A swing trader, particularly for international exchange as well as stock index sector, can go both short or long to take every chance. Additionally, it means, inside a trading week, when a market place is volatile, a swing trader can come across many trading potentials he or maybe she is able to capture.

Made in the USA
Monee, IL
11 December 2020